Touching Cloth

*Confessions and communions
of a young priest*

www.penguin.co.uk

Touching Cloth

Confessions and communions
of a young priest

THE REVEREND FERGUS
BUTLER-GALLIE

bantam

TRANSWORLD PUBLISHERS
Penguin Random House, One Embassy Gardens,
8 Viaduct Gardens, London SW11 7BW
www.penguin.co.uk

Transworld is part of the Penguin Random House group of companies
whose addresses can be found at global.penguinrandomhouse.com

First published in Great Britain in 2023 by Bantam
an imprint of Transworld Publishers

A CIP catalogue record for this book
is available from the British Library.

ISBN 9781787635753

Typeset in 12/15pt Bembo Book MT Pro by Jouve (UK), Milton Keynes.
Printed and bound in Great Britain by Clays Ltd, Elcograf S.p.A.

The authorized representative in the EEA is Penguin Random House Ireland,
Morrison Chambers, 32 Nassau Street, Dublin D02 YH68.

Penguin Random House is committed to a sustainable future
for our business, our readers and our planet. This book is made
from Forest Stewardship Council® certified paper.

To my parents, with gratitude and love

Contents

Author's Note

St Laurence is one of my favourite saints, primarily because he had a sense of humour. Those whom the Church designates saintly are, of course, flesh and blood but their humanity can, so often, disappear behind a veneer of holy perfection. Not so Laurence. Even when he was martyred – by being roasted alive on a grill – he couldn't resist making a joke.

'Turn me over!' he cried to his executioners. 'I'm done on this side!'

The event that got him into trouble was a more practical joke and, like all the best jokes of that genre, one that taught a valuable lesson. It was said that, when ordered by the emperor to array the treasures of the Church for inspection (and, presumably, confiscation) he gathered together not gold or silver but people. Lame, sick and old people. Young, unknown and irrelevant people. Odd, erratic and irritating people. These, Laurence claimed to the bemused imperial guard, were the true treasures of the Church.

I'm as susceptible to a piece of Georgian silver as the next cleric but I agree with him. In a faith that believes God became human, people are always going to be considered our greatest treasure and joy. Consequently, this book is full of them. No confidences have been compromised, and all those who are named or directly identifiable have had sight of the text before publication. It is my sincere hope that my jokes in the tradition of Laurence have not compromised the sense of these remarkable people as treasure in my or God's eyes.

Introduction

'What made you become a priest?'

As with almost all open-ended questions, this one gets asked with a ready-made answer already firmly in the mind of the interrogator. I've been asked it many times by many people. In pubs (once, memorably, before a man sicked seven or eight pints' worth of Foster's all over himself), at dinners (I am 90 per cent sure I was invited to at least one dinner party to distract from the hosting couple's impending break-up), by people in the street, by members of my congregation. I've been asked more times than I can count. Over the years I've realized that it's really several different questions, and expects several different answers, depending on where the questioner puts their emphasis.

'What made you become a *priest*?' That's the tone adopted by a kindly stranger at a house party or drinks event when they learn what I do. It's almost always a precursor to a prolonged sharing of their, often hostile, attitude to religion while I try desperately to catch eyes with someone who might swoop in and change the subject. They almost always carry the vague, lager-fuelled hope that they – the brother of the girlfriend of someone I knew at university – might finally turn me from the error of my ways. Oh, to have such faith!

'What made *you* become a priest?' This is asked by one of two types of people. First, a disappointed bottomless bruncher, who hoped that being young(ish) and male and in a pub frequented by hen dos meant I might otherwise have been fair game (of course, the aftermath of a bottomless brunch is perhaps not the right time to explain that the Church of England takes a more relaxed approach to clerical celibacy than Rome). Or, sadly more realistically, and certainly far more often, by my mother: in response to some word of manifestly unchristian venom shot at a sibling or an example of ungodly personal cleanliness.

'What made you *become* a priest?' A knottier, more difficult question, asked by wise vicars of many years' standing, or by my fraught conscience of a sleepless night, and one I struggle to answer. 'Becoming' hardly suggests something that happens overnight. Does anyone ever really grow into a role like mine? Can anyone truly become the priest they should be, least of all someone who first becomes so in their mid-twenties? At what point does one truly *become* a priest? Am I there yet? How can someone who can't even remember Euro '96 or can still recall a playground grudge over Pokémon cards (I'm looking at you, Charlie) speak of life and death, love and beauty, Heaven and God? How can *anyone* speak convincingly of the Divine to a world that seems quite as far from it as this one?

Fear not, however, dear reader. This is not some existentialist treatise. Coward that I am, I normally defuse each and every one of these questions with humour.

Taking a deep breath, I pretend to consider the question long and hard. I might allow my eyes to flit ever so briefly upwards as if I were a prophet of old seeking to invoke Divine wisdom, before uttering, 'Well, I heard that black was slimming!'

The questioner will smirk and nod, their question expertly evaded. Occasionally, if they're feeling generous, I might even elicit a chuckle. It's a great get-out-of-jail-free response. We can move on to simpler things – houseplant maintenance, a friend's latest dating mishaps, the meaning of life – and it has the advantage of being true: clerical wear really is slimming. Although not, perhaps, for the reasons you might expect. But we'll get to that later. In the meantime, welcome to a year in the life of a young, unlikely, unexpected, and frankly unprepared priest.

I.

Death and the Summer

It was one of those airless afternoons in the heat of mid-August, not long after I had been ordained. The tarmac shimmered, allowing the cul-de-sacs of north Liverpool to dream they might be Arizona freeways – and I was on my way to greet a dead man. I was still getting used to my cassock. It is a black woollen garment, designed to imbue me with the weight of my calling and stymied any attempt at severe clerical dignity. I might as well have been wearing a bin bag. Black, then, truly was slimming, in the way that hot yoga is slimming. My briny essence poured from my brow as I walked to the house where our appointment was to take place. There I was, trying to muster all the solemnity required for funeral ministry, and I looked like I'd just slid head-first down a log flume.

Louis, our pastoral assistant, had kindly but, as it would turn out, foolishly come along to help with the liturgy. We were there for a 'lying-in': the practice of saying prayers over a body that has been brought back into the family home prior to the funeral, which in this case was two days later. In some parts of Liverpool, where I served my first post, death is a public business. There is no bourgeois, privatized grief in Kirkby or Everton or Anfield. Dying and its after-effects remain ritualized in these terraced back-streets – meaning that, when the eternal beckons, every former docker or cabbie is treated like a minor royal, and every two-up two-down becomes, for a day or so, Westminster Abbey. The deceased is brought home, the 'sheets' are put up,* and family and friends flock to pay their respects. Death, in short, is met with those ever-open Scouse arms of welcome, and carried, quite literally, into the front room. It's an admirably forthright way of dealing with that which must meet us all, and strikes me as far healthier than a Home Counties 'Life Celebration' at a faceless suburban crem.

A crowd swelled outside the house. It looked as if the whole postcode was present: it was rammed out the

---

* Quite literally bed sheets draped around the front room of the house, creating a makeshift chapel of rest in the midst of the family home. Fairy lights, football scarves, *objets* of a faith now rediscovered are all arranged to create a space where the living and the dead mingle freely, children popping in and out to see their grandparent or uncle with an admirable nonchalance. This not being a practice I had encountered in my childhood (where extended family – regardless of their state of decomposition – were kept at a distance), I must say that on my first such visit to a lying-in I was under the distinct impression that I was entering a macabre Santa's grotto.

front, down the alley to the side, in the garden. As I passed through – dabbing at the Niagara Falls emanating from my brow while trying to respond to every 'Hello, Father', 'Thanks for coming, Father,' and 'God bless, Father' – I found the inside even busier. There was beer and smoking, and I fielded a few winking 'Very young for a vicar' shots from matriarchs ensconced in chairs at key points along the route. It was not a conventional funereal atmosphere, with rosé closer to hand than rosaries. Rather, family and friends had gathered together as they would at a birthday or barbecue or – although, I confess, not my area of expertise – bar mitzvah. The only difference was that one of the guests was dead.

I was shown through to the room where the deceased lay. It had been agreed that I would say some prayers to start off the formal process of commending a soul to God, then lead a recitation of the Rosary. The sheets were well and truly up, the room immaculately decorated. It wasn't a large space but it was full of the paraphernalia of a life – photos with children and grandchildren, trinkets from holidays long past – and the paraphernalia of death: cards, flowers, the air of 'deepest sympathy'.

It was also full of people. There were, by my reckoning, about fifteen mourners already squeezed in round the edges of the room and only the smallest crack in the window through which any fresh air could enter. I looked to the body, to the crack in the window, to the book that contained the prayers and finally behind me, where a gathering crowd had clearly realized the main event was about to occur. It was a case of now or never, so I launched in: 'Our Father, which art in Heaven . . .'

'He's doing the prayers!'

This rippled back through the assembled crowd, initially in a whisper but becoming progressively louder as it reached the outer circle (accompanied, with a good Scouse sense of irony, by a loud 'SHUSH'). It became noticeably hotter as people piled in as subtly as they might. Still, from a selfish point of view, our little clerical party was facing away from this crowd, so I had a monopoly on the weak but much-needed waft of air through the solitary chink in the window.

The Rosary – for those readers not totally up to date with their popular Catholic devotional practices – consists of five 'decades': sets of ten recitations of the prayer beginning 'Hail Mary, full of grace, the Lord is with thee'. Each one is interspersed with further prayers. In the stifling heat, time had taken on a slower pace and 'decade' began to feel a little too literal. It was, I think, at the midpoint of the second decade when I began to notice that through the crack a faint but definite wisp of smoke had begun to dance. This was followed by – to someone who had spent his early twenties living in the back-streets of Prague – an all too familiar smell.

Uh-oh. That's weed, went my brain.

'Hail Mary, full of grace, the Lord is with thee,' continued my lips.

Now, 'Judge not lest ye be judged' is at the heart of the Christian faith, and you haven't picked up this book to read a prolonged treatise against recreational drug use.

Indeed, I can even see why the person had chosen this specific area to light a joint. To a passer-by, the living room looked unoccupied, with light-cancelling blinds: the perfect venue for a brief narcotic foray.

Unfortunately, none of this Christian charity helped solve the problem in front of me – namely that I was in danger of presiding over an elaborate hotboxing incident.* As a young priest, this is not the kind of nightmare you anticipate: leaving a group of elderly, bereaved people not with a sense of being comforted as they mourned but instead as high as kites.

As I was the only one directly in the path of the offending billow, I considered whether I could change the direction of the smoke between the prayers. I concluded that blowing marijuana smoke over a body was probably not the best look for a cleric. My eyes darted to Louis. He had noticed it too. Cue frantic work by our respective facial features as we tried to communicate non-verbally while maintaining the dignity required.

I need scarcely mention how this second development had affected the sweating situation. The perspiration had now drenched my brow and was stinging my eyes. My cassock clung to me like an all-in-one Lycra exercise suit. The gusset of my boxer shorts— Let's not go there.

In the end, I decided to speed up the Hail Marys. To its

---

* The practice of minimizing the airflow in and out of a particular space to render the mood-changing smoke of particular narcotics more efficacious. Or so it says here anyway.

credit, the congregation kept up. Afterwards many remarked how it was good to do things 'properly' and that this was precisely what the deceased would have wanted. Considering the occasion, they were all in quite a good mood.

In future years, I would do multiple funerals with only a small congregation. Sometimes it was just me, the corpse, the undertaker and the angels. This almost carnival atmosphere was different, testament, I think, to the power of community in the midst of adversity. Something about hearing laughter mingled with tears spoke of the strength of the people gathered there, and sharing memories inevitably mixes grief and joy.

I said my goodbyes, comforted where I could, and retrieved a wad of red paper napkins from under a pile of sausage rolls to dab my moistened brow. Then, navigating the crowds, I made my way out into the sweltering afternoon. From there I wandered back to the church, contemplating death with (as I later discovered) pastry stuck to my forehead and God only knows what in my lungs.

†

All clergy have anecdotes about death. There are two reasons for this. First, death, even when it happens to others, does strange things to people, leading them to behaviour that is . . . Shall we say conspicuous? Second, it's something we all have to face eventually so it seems only sensible to observe how others cope with it. That's not to say all of us are affected by death in the same way. For some it's the last dread terror while others greet it like an old friend.

My mother, a doctor who has dealt with death for some years, once observed that the clergy she encountered all appeared to be either hypochondriacs or hedonists. While the former seemed terrified of edging closer to the eternal, the latter embraced the bottle, tobacco or the mountains of baked goods parishioners tend to offer with such gusto as to meet their Maker sooner than He might have intended.* Of course, being around death all the time means that priests can't claim to be surprised by it. In fact, you might have thought that all that studying and preaching about God and eternal life would hone our instincts on the afterlife. In truth, all deaths hit in a different way, and many are still moments of deep pain, no matter how robust an individual priest's faith in the afterlife may be.

To my mind, the best attitude for a Christian, and especially a priest, is to face death with a mocking glee. I will never forget the attitude of one elderly lady I met while I was training for ministry. I was in Rome, at a sort of Church of England embassy. It was the height of summer and – to continue a theme – swelteringly hot. This, though, was before the solemn dignity of orders had led me to possess the sort of all-black wardrobe Ozzy Osbourne might like, so I spent my days on a small

---

* This, of course, compromises the omniscience of God and so must therefore be taken as a joke.

internal balcony of a palazzo near the Forum, wearing shorts.

Every Wednesday, just before midday, a coiffured vision in a twin set and pearls would burst in and holler, in a broad transatlantic drawl, 'Nice shorts, Fergie! I *love* your legs.' Being catcalled by eighty-somethings is not what they train you for in theological college. She had been a society beauty, married to an Italian aristocrat. He had died young, which freed her, like a character in a Noël Coward song, to live the sort of life you always assume only exists in novels. Yet it had not been without gilded tragedy. When a priest famously asked her how such a long widowhood had affected her, she looked away from him and said, in that cut-glass drawl, 'Losing my husband was the worst thing that ever happened to me . . .' Cue a long draw on a cigarette, followed by a swivel of the head to fix the priest with her gaze. '. . . and the *best*.' Hers was an infectious *joie de vivre* that wasn't going to let the petty inevitability of dying get in the way.

Most people engage with death rarely and only when absolutely necessary, but for the clergy, it may crop up three times a week during 'the funeral season'. It might not be something we especially wish to dwell on, but there are always times of the year, as excessive cold or heat sets in, that result in a higher number of funerals. It isn't that people *don't* die during the rest of the year but rather that there are times when more people reach the end of their earthly sojourn than at others. Put another way, very few undertakers book a holiday in January.

Like undertakers, your average vicar is well attuned to the reality and regularity of death, so a lexicon of stories – tales, myths, anecdotes – has risen around it. Consequently I, like most clergy, have thought about how I should like to go: clinging on, embittered, in a four-poster bed, while a howling storm rages and a cast of grotesque relatives sit in icy tension on the other side of a thick oak door. Sadly, death's not something we ordinarily get a huge amount of choice in. What can be said is that no two brushes with death are comparable, no two griefs or stories of parting identical.

Many are deeply moving – families bereft of those who died too young, or tragically, or without warning. There are stories of sparsely attended 'Eleanor Rigby'-style goodbyes, with a handful of mourners huddled round a grave to commend a soul, still precious regardless, to God.*

That said, in death tragedy and comedy are never too far from one another. I remember one of the first times I anointed someone on their deathbed. I arrived at a care home with, I was told, little time to spare. I was met not by doctors or family but with a procession headed by a man engaged in a series of determined attempts to pull

---

* It is not my place to tell tales of lockdown funerals in 2020, though I did oversee some. It is my sincere hope that, while ministry at the bedside was in the brave and capable hands of doctors, chaplains, nurses and porters, we – parish clergy, undertakers, relatives – managed to afford a quiet dignity to those distanced farewells, despite the many challenges that stood in our way.

his trousers down. Each time he succeeded, the staff following him along the corridor would rush forward and pull them up again. I allowed this strange picaresque to pass, let myself into the relevant room, and there prayed in an atmosphere of tangibly holy calm as a family bade a quiet, expected but still sad goodbye.

Some clergy tell stories with a gallows humour darker than any cassock, such as the vicar who witnessed a gravedigger keeling over dead into the hole he had just dug. Grimmer still, an unsuspecting clergyman found himself an inadvertent accessory to crime when one mourner used a funeral as cover to murder another. Most, however, are more comforting tales of errors and foibles that serve as reminders of our humanity.

A funeral early in my ministry in Liverpool was supposed to begin – as so many do for men of a certain age – with 'My Way' playing as the coffin entered. However, a mix-up by the family meant that the body was instead carried in to another Sinatra hit, 'I've Got You Under My Skin', which was, I suppose, a more technically accurate musical representation of post-mortem processes, if not exactly what the mourners had intended. Another involved the reading of a poem entitled 'I'm Free'. It's a meditation on the release that death can sometimes bring for those suffering but the person allocated to read it was gloriously camp in his approach, delivery and exit. It was rather like having a eulogy delivered by a pantomime dame. Observing these natural moments of comedy or irony isn't a mark of disrespect – except, perhaps, to Death, who, we must imagine, isn't too keen on

anyone laughing in his face. A funeral, for all its sombre-
ness, is a gathering of people, fallible and funny as they
are.

As a child, long before any sense of belief dawned
upon me, I attended my grandfather's. I remember thinking how strange it was to see my grandmother, a woman
for whom the word 'robust' was specifically created, in
tears. It was even stranger to see my father and his brother,
who had fallen out over some dogs around 1994, making
polite small-talk over post-crematorium caviar. No surprise, then, that funerals were always, in my mind, a
journey into the topsy-turvy.

My own favourite funeral story is comparatively tame
in comparison to many. Many of the potential pitfalls
come, from the priest's point of view, in what goes on
around the funeral rather than during the service. The
weight of emotion, the dignity of the liturgy and the
grace of God will get you through the forty minutes in
church, but they won't help you remember to ensure
your flies are done up at the wake or get you to the crematorium on time. In the latter case, undertakers are a huge
help (they may well be in the former case as well but,
thankfully, I've never tested them).

During one service, I had hitched a ride with the
hearse from the church to the crematorium where we
were to perform the committal of the body. I was sitting
in the front of the vehicle, draped in black, next to the
driver, also draped in black, as we drove slowly behind a
senior funeral director. We inched along at her walking
pace, as if we were in a lorry crawling over black ice. The

procession was suitably stately. This was in a part of town where funeral cortèges were not uncommon – a hazard of playing host to a crematorium, you might say – and were always treated with ceremony and respect. Cars would slow down, signs of the Cross would be made, baseball caps removed, and pedestrians would often stand still. All reasonable responses to encountering a reminder of our shared mortality while on your way to Tesco.

That day was no different in many respects – signs of the Cross were made, hats removed and a couple of pedestrians indeed slowed down. To a halt, in fact, just as the hearse stopped at a red light. The pair, with a physical size disparity that would have been at home on a seaside postcard of a less enlightened era, were clad in jogging gear. They took in the scene in quiet contemplation. Then the silence of the afternoon was broken as the woman cried to the man, 'That's it – I've had enough! Fuck the couch and fuck the five K!'

I turned, the driver turned, the senior funeral director turned. Behind us, in the limousine in which the family were sat, several heads turned as well. It wasn't the most conventional way to break the pre-cremation tension, but it was a strangely appropriate reminder of living earthiness before I pronounced, 'Ashes to ashes, dust to dust . . .'

†

Clergy aren't alone in needing something to smile about in the face of death: doctors, soldiers, police and undertakers are all part of the same quiet club. We may encounter it regularly but we still feel the pang of each loss and never become unable to grieve. Instead we develop coping mechanisms, one of which is, of course, sharing glances, nods, stories, sighs with others who go through it frequently.

This often shows during hospital visits. I have shared glances that pitch themselves between respectful resignation and cheery solidarity with nurses as I made my way through the Emergency Resuscitation Suite. Perhaps our association with death is why so many people – normal people, I mean – fear doctors or priests. We're reminders of mortality. I suppose there are people who fear both for other reasons – the demonically possessed or Members of Parliament, for example – but we shan't dwell on them here.

Part of it is perhaps born of clergy wearing black clothing. I was never going to be one of those vicars who shoehorn a bit of white plastic into a Hawaiian shirt, least of all when visiting a hospital, but I still try not to cultivate the angel-of-death look, offsetting my sombre dress with a smile. It doesn't always pay off.

On one occasion, I swept into a ward to visit a parishioner who'd undergone routine care and was soon to be discharged. Understandably, in that world of Lucozade, bedpans and bleeping monitors, they needed a bit of cheering up. There were four beds: one with my intended visitee, one filled with a shapeless sleeping form and then, on the other side of the room, two beds in which sat gaunt men of indeterminate age.

'Oho! Father's here. Someone's really done for now!' the man on the right gargled, only half joking.

'Oh, no, we're all right,' counselled the one on the left. 'Doctors – fine. Priests – fine. It's when you get a visit from the lawyers that you know you're fucked.'

It was comforting to discover that there was at least one profession more feared and disliked than the clergy.

†

The difference between priests and other professional harbingers of death is, I suppose, that we are contractually obliged to throw in a caveat: that death is not the end. In fact, it's a beginning. Death might seem a peculiar place to start a book, but for someone in this line of work it makes total sense. Unless you're a cat or James Bond, death only happens once, but for priests, we sign up to death – or, more accurately, the promise that we will die – on the morning of our ordination and every day thereafter.

Ordinations almost always happen in the summer – although some occur in late September, just as the shops prepare for the plastic death orgy of Halloween. Both seasons are appropriate in their way. Slavic folklore holds a summer's day as the domain of Lady Midday, who, clad in a long white robe, approaches the young and naive and calls them to die. In the noonday heat in Liverpool one June, I, too, was approached by a figure in a long white robe and called to die. The difference was that this was an invitation to life *through* death – plus the Bishop of Liverpool had a beard and doesn't like being called Lady Midday.

Ordination is a strange business – part minutiae-filled legal procedure, part joyful celebration, part terrifying stare over the precipice of the rest of your life. Ordinations tend to occur in cathedrals: those titanic sermons in stone are designed to imbue us with a sense of the awesomeness of God, and the feeling that – not unlike your first kiss, or last tax bill – you are standing at the edge of something of huge, cosmic import. There are less formal celebrations afterwards: mine was in a pub basement and resulted in a clergyman being indecently assaulted (of which more later).

In past years, aware of the potential for alcohol and good company to soothe nerves, bishops used to treat their soon-to-be clergy to wine-soaked last suppers for their lay status, meaning that many clergy actually had the Holy Spirit imparted to them while their bloodstream coursed with an earthly spirit. Nowadays such extravagances are sadly gone, replaced by sandwiches (if you're lucky) and angst. That is not to say some clergy don't still manage to bid adieu to ordinary life with a glug of something potent. Before my own, I remember asking one friend at his service how it felt now to be ordained. Having sourced various spirits the night before and sporting a headache to match, he replied that he felt like he was at his own funeral.

I had not dissimilar feelings when I was ordained. Not,

alas, because I had succeeded in drinking anything more than a pint or two the night before. We were in a dry retreat house in Wales and a group of us had managed to escape to the local pub. Nevertheless, that summer the end of one life lay heavily on my shoulders as I placed the stole over them for the first time.*

Of course I wasn't actually dying – I would still be able to eat, drink and breathe. I wasn't even becoming a monk – I could marry and talk and meet up with friends. But what changed that afternoon in Liverpool was how people saw me. I was no longer just *me*, a young man who liked beer and lie-ins and stupid videos of people letting off air horns on golf courses but, for better or worse, a symbol of hope to some and hate to others. The old unencumbered me was gone: I had vowed to do and be something more. I'd promised to 'die to self and live to Christ and my neighbour'.

Of course I failed. Indeed, I still fail in this. All clergy do. I fail to die to self when I conceal my collar because I haven't got the cash on me to buy a *Big Issue*; when I

---

* The stole is a long thin piece of embroidered material draped round one shoulder, like a beauty queen's sash, when you're made a deacon, and round your neck when you're ordained a priest. The origin and symbolism of the stole is the subject of much debate. Some link it to the cloth Jesus used to wash the feet of the disciples at the Last Supper, others to a Jewish prayer shawl, while the most convincing is that it was a mark of status for middle-ranking Roman officials. Whether it was originally a shawl, an ancient local councillor's sash or a glorified tea towel is sort of irrelevant. It now serves as a mark of holy orders.

secretly cheer the misfortune of some imagined enemy; when I get off the bus a stop early to avoid a barrage of questions about life, death (normally of pets) and the universe from those who love to strike up conversations on public transport; when I recall all the drinks I had at a university party in 2013 instead of listening to a sermon; whenever I go on Twitter; when I let irritation or hate or lust or envy or avarice bubble up inside me. In short, I'm called to make God known while being all too human.

All this makes it sound a bit like a punishment arranged by the Greek gods on Olympus: 'Eee – that Butler-Gallie's a right cocky sod. What we got in store fer 'im?' (I don't know about you but I imagine the Ancient Greek pantheon being composed of characters from the glory days of *Coronation Street*.)

''Ow about a lifetime of being asked whether budgies go to Heaven by strangers on buses?'

'Perfick.'

But it isn't a punishment at all. Being ordained was – is – a privilege and a joy and, crucially, as I am contractually obliged to tell you, it leads me to a fuller, more joyous life. It doesn't always feel like that when an alarm goes off at 6 a.m. on a Sunday morning or when someone manages to piss down the walls of the church loo or when I'm dealing with the cold dead hand of the central Church of England but there can be no denying that, as a priest, my life feels richer and happier than it would if I weren't. And much of that fulfilment has come about as a result of promising to die to self. Starting this tale of priesthood with death, then, seems natural. After all, Christianity started with a death – that is, a death that was life that was a death (of Death). But let's not go into that just yet.

So, to answer the original question, what *did* make me become a priest?

Death, I suppose.

2.

A Small Piece of Cloth

GROWING INTO MINISTRY

Sometimes I wonder which is the most-told parental lie. That parents deceive their offspring is no secret – but the frequency of specific deceits must surely be quantifiable. For instance, I imagine few parents are psychopathic enough to tell children that their grandmother is dead only for her to turn up to Sunday lunch, but many will have mumbled something about storks or stars or special cuddles when asked to explain how a new brother or sister came to be.

I think 'You'll grow into it' was probably the most egregious and oft-repeated untruth of my childhood and one that followed me into priesthood.* Just before I was ordained I set about buying the bits of linen that were to become the key indicators of my identity for the

---

* Honourable mentions going to 'You'll enjoy it', 'Only for five more minutes' and 'No, we don't have a favourite.'

following decades. Some clergy opt for plastic slip-ins, but I tried one once and found it to be exactly as uncomfortable as it sounds. So, along with stockbrokers, barristers, and people who have recently awoken from comas acquired in the 1980s, I elected for shirts with a detachable linen or cotton collar. Collar sizes, of course, are especially deceitful among men. A shirt that was once loose-fitting, airy even, can turn traitor and become chokingly tight around the neck, doling out vigilante justice for the crime of too many biscuits. As I was being measured in a specialist store for clerical clothing, I was made horribly aware of this as I realized I would have to repurchase them at half-inch intervals as the inexorable march of my well-earned jowls continued apace.

I discussed my quandary with an experienced priest, mentioning that deliveries of cakes from kind parishioners and the attendance at drinks receptions expected by local dignitaries probably meant that the moment of tightness at the neck might happen sooner rather than later. He agreed that a little room in that area might be judicious, before adding, while smiling the smile of the aged and venerable when dispensing wisdom to the young, 'Of course, you never *really* grow into the collar at all.'

It was good advice. All the above instances of collar-inspired interaction occurred during my first three years of wearing one. I'm not sure what the next thirty or more will bring, but I think it unlikely that I will have 'grown into' the collar to the point at which I'm unsurprised by the trust and openness, kindness, venom and straightforward good old-fashioned lunacy that a little strip of cloth or plastic can attract.

†

'Scuse me. Are you a priest?'

It's September, and I'm clad from head to foot in black, with the exception of a large, starched white linen collar, and walking down the pathway next to the church. While this might seem like asking someone wearing scrubs in a hospital if they're a doctor, or if the person floating weightlessly in the International Space Station is an astronaut, in fairness to him, I might conceivably have been a very ugly stripper.

'I am! How can I help?'

'I got a question.'

I begin to root frantically through the rusted filing cabinets of my brain to find the neatly typed mental memo titled 'How to Explain the Problem of Evil in an Accessible Way'. I also hunt scrawled Post-it notes with 'Yes, we can get married', 'No, we're not all paedos' and 'Yes, I do think there were five thousand of them' for deployment.

'You've got a whole *round* white bit round your neck, but some priests just have those little bits there.' He points to the spot underneath his Adam's apple. 'What's all that about?'

It's a salutary lesson. Clergy like to think that people will be intrigued by our otherworldliness (though I confess, I'm probably not the most likely candidate to be accused of possessing that particular virtue), but all this man wanted to explore was my choice of accessories. When one is used to dealing with the extremes of human experience, it becomes tempting to view every member of the general public as a living, breathing bag of existential angst, to imagine that they're desperate to unload their problems, hopes or fears on someone who is signalling themselves as a listening ear. This man simply saw someone in a weird outfit and asked him about it. Good on him.

Had a cleric seen me, it would have been different. They would immediately have been able to detect that the particular style of collar I wore, and the particular way I wore it, indicated a preference for worship using the Book of Common Prayer over Common Worship, for sherry rather than gin, and for rugby over football.* Such are the signals vicars send each other. Any event filled with clergy will feature every array of outfit possible, from those who deliberately never wear any form of identifying clerical clothing, to outfits so extravagant they make Liberace look like an odd-job man.

When most people see someone in a dog collar (a phrase that apparently began as a term of sartorial abuse

---

* Frankly, when it comes to Common Worship (the Church of England's famously complex and supposedly more accessible liturgy devised in 2000), while I'm sure it does it for some people, I'd rather praise God using a dishwasher manual.

by one wing of the Church towards another), they make the very reasonable baseline assumption that that person is a Christian, a professional one no less. This assumption tells them that we're qualified to give directions to a railway station without sending them in the opposite direction for a laugh, that we will most probably spare what change we might have for the needy, and that we can answer the very deepest questions about life and death. Although, thinking about it, I wouldn't trust some of us on the railway station.

That is not to say everyone wishes to take us up on those qualifications. For the vast majority of people, just knowing what we do is plenty of religious contact, thank you very much. Indeed, there's a particular smile that many people shoot at us clergy – a curious tensing of the face that, while conforming to the technical definition of a smile, is really more of a nervous gurn. It's an upwards contortion of the lips that acknowledges us in a positive way but also sets a boundary, a not-quite-grin that says, 'Hello, yes, good for you, please don't talk to me about death, see you at Christmas.' In short, it's the sort of face you'd pull at someone who *could* turn you into a frog but who you were 99.9 per cent sure was too nice to do so.

As one of the vast swathe of ordinary and non-photogenic people who make up the majority of the population, I was used to slipping into the background. Now, I was very noticeably *visible*. Whether I liked it or not, eyes were instinctively drawn to me. Not in the way they're drawn to a society beauty or a rock star, of course,

closer to the way in which they're drawn to an embar-
rassingly dressed groom-to-be on a stag do. However,
there have been times when that bit of white fabric has
given me permission to act in what I'd hope was a Christian manner.

One day, as autumn was just flirting with the idea of
beginning his ravages properly, and to further my vague
sense of being an imposter, I was standing outside a
church that wasn't my own. Imposter syndrome is a
very real thing for clergy – unsurprising, perhaps, since
our ultimate boss is God, whose intangible, incompar-
able majesty it is our job to make known in no more
than about fifty-five minutes once a week. In those
early months after I was ordained I found it hard not to
believe that a TV crew were going to appear during a
sermon and announce it was all an elaborate practical
joke. However, this ecclesiastical loitering with intent
wasn't, you understand, a stakeout or an attempt at
passing myself off as the vicar. I was there to take part in
a social-action project, the term we now use for feeding
the hungry, clothing the naked, welcoming the stranger,
whatever.

Those seeking help at that church were from a panoply of different countries due to its vicinity to a
boarding house where the Home Office sent people
prior to deportation. Despite the sheer number of
people who were waiting outside, a queue had formed –
polite, almost silent, orderly – that would have done any
Home Counties' garden centre proud. Collar still
starched and fresh white, I was tasked with greeting

people and ensuring they knew where to queue (such was the perceived importance of the queuing system), and where to enter to get the help they needed. For most this was a bag or two of food to get them through the following week but for others it was a pack of toiletries, a new pair of shoes or a pack of nappies. Of all the people in the world, you could forgive them desperation – some had only the clothes they stood up in – yet in front of me stood a long line of people, all firing the same awkward smile in my direction. Cultural assimilation at its very finest.*

This modern British idyll was interrupted by a noise like a motorbike being unwillingly cajoled into turning a corner at great speed. When the source of the noise finally hove into view from around the corner of the church, it proved, impressively, to be human, not mechanical. A group of three men appeared who, although they were extravagantly bearded, were clearly neither members of a biker gang nor of the Orthodox priesthood. It soon became clear that the fascinating mechanical voice belonged to the stockiest and shortest figure in the middle of the trio. His friends joined the queue, continuing their whooping, while this gentleman, who had

---

* Though it ought to be noted that many of these men and women came from countries where the clergy could have had them arrested or whipped or hanged. While the National Secular Society seems convinced that the Archbishop of Canterbury and the Ayatollah are the same, a cursory discussion with those queuing on that and other days confirms that they're very much not.

spotted my collar, made a beeline for me and placed himself firmly in front of me, about four inches from my face
to be exact.

'Scuse me, are you a priest?' he asked. (I begin to think
that maybe mine is a face that says 'cobbler', 'newsagent'
or 'arms dealer' rather than 'vicar'.)

'Well, I'm ordained,' I replied, thinking immediately
that it was probably not the time to bring up the onto-
logical differences between orders of the clergy.

Once again my mind rattled – as it always does –
through what he might want. To my shame, it turned
instinctively to money.

Instead he placed his hand on my arm, turning us
both away from the gaze of the line, and asked, his
almost mechanical rasp much softer now, if I could say a
prayer for him. I bowed my head, noticing the contrast
of my feet, shod in black leather, and his, the side of a
trainer split to reveal bare skin. I prayed that he might be
guarded and guided over the course of that day. We
rounded off on the same Amen, looked up and smiled at
one another.

'Thank you, Father,' he rasped.

'No – thank *you*,' I replied.

You might view such an encounter as merely transac-
tional, but if it was I got so much more out of it. My
morning full of awkward gurning at strangers was
rewarded, and a degree of purpose restored. All this,
courtesy of a man who sounded like a motorbike. But to
view it like that would be a mistake. In reality it was a
chance to do something that we are rarely given

permission to do due to busyness, social norms, or whatever it is that makes most people pull that awkward smile:
to strike up a momentary and meaningful relationship
with someone I'd never met before, and may never meet
again. And all that initiated and enabled by a weird bit of
starched fabric round my neck.

After the programme had finished, and the queue dis-
seminated, I walked back towards the city centre with a
distinct spring in my step. Perhaps this was the right calling. Perhaps I wasn't such an imposter as I'd thought.
Perhaps the prank TV crew had bigger fish to fry. I came
to a pedestrian crossing and waited, so lost in my smug
rumination on vocation that I scarcely noticed the man –
about my age or slightly younger – in high-vis overalls
standing next to me. He eyed my collar before carefully
removing his headphones.

'So, have you been to the vet or something?'

God rarely allows pride to linger for too long and I
continue to wonder whether the Channel 5 camera will
appear one day, after all.

†

One of the strange aspects about putting on a clerical collar is that people start inviting you to things. This isn't to
say I was the sort of kid whose parents had to beg other
children to spend time with him, although I can think of
certain grown-ups from my childhood years who would
have preferred that I wasn't invited round to their houses
for games of indoor football with their offspring. Still, it

was quite a shock to have people you'd barely met kindly invite you to spend often prolonged periods with them. You soon realize that every lunch in a dog collar is a working lunch. In those early months after ordination, I was inundated with invites to lunch at a restaurant, lunch at home, even to share one packed lunch on a bus, all by kindly congregation members as a sort of a 'welcome to the parish'.

Incidentally, I love a lunch: a proper lunch, that is. In fact, there's a delicious (and I use that word shamelessly) irony in that the very best lunches cease to be lunches at all, long into the normal domain of tea or dinner or sometimes supper. There's something satisfyingly decadent – a little transgressive, even – about having a bottle of wine in the middle of the day. It is an act normally reserved for times of organized misrule, like holidays, or Christmas, or three years at a theological college. It's a luxury that seems even naughtier when you're wearing a dog collar.

That said, for all the limitations you feel the dog collar brings, I have, once or twice, heard stories of members of the Church going overboard with regard to food and drink. One of the greatest joys of those early months of ministry was getting to know the selection of people, mostly the elderly and the housebound, who could not routinely make it to church. In these cases church, in the form of Holy Communion and my wittering conversation, came to them. One of the most colourful of this palette of characters was Marge, a great Evertonian bumper of generous humanity who would sit in her chair and chuckle away at stories garnered from near ninety years well lived. A favourite such tale of hers dated from the early 1990s, when she had been a churchwarden. After a small, informal Communion service one Saturday morning she took the then rector aside. 'There's a nun sat outside the church. I saw her when I came in,' she informed him.

'Oh, yes?' (This is a convenient, catch-all response to pieces of information proffered without further explanation at the end of church services, and one I confess to having deployed a number of times.)

'She's drunk,' Marge told the rector, with – if her telling of it in later years is anything to go by – barely disguised glee.

'Oh, yes?' (While this response is helpful in its time and place, it does have a tendency to become something of a clerical verbal tic.) 'How could you tell?'

'Well,' continued Marge, 'when I wished her a good morning, she told me to fuck off.'

Cue a cackle from Marge and the assembled company.

When I assisted at her funeral, held in the midst of that distanced year, the few who were able to come spent the service and after sharing many such stories. Like so many of her generous generation, she was a great bringer of cheek and joy and, in the case of the drunken nun, a valuable lesson about the perils of assuming external religiosity.

Theology of abstinence aside, clergy rarely have time to indulge in Hogarthian sessions at the buffet any more. In fact, clerical eating patterns are, in my experience, positively deranged. Black may be slimming but the habit of eating whatever you can whenever you can certainly isn't. It was something I began to notice within the first month or two as the bin in my office, the pockets of my jacket, even, at one point, a drawer in the sacristy, filled with the tell-tale paraphernalia of lunches on the move: a Monster Munch packet hidden in the folds of some vestments, a Cheestring wrapper secreted in an order of service, that sort of thing. By way of an experiment, I noted down my lunch pattern for a totally unremarkable, average week in the midst of September:

MONDAY: a mouthful of Cheddar and a corni-chon (an ill-fated attempt at a ploughman's grazed direct from the fridge, sadly interrupted by a text reminding me I was supposed to be assisting at a lunchtime Communion service).

TUESDAY: three packets of aerated potato bears (the sole bounty to be had from a suburban railway-station vending machine, wolfed down to the anguished stares of my fellow travellers on a train back from a pastoral visit on the edge of the city).

WEDNESDAY: potted crab, butterfly breast of chicken, Eton mess, cheeseboard, glass of Rioja (part of an official function at which I said grace and gave a short speech – impossible to say if resultant indigestion was the result of the crab or the small-talk).

THURSDAY: nothing (the day when I was most often involved in church projects to feed the hungry was, ironically, also the part of the week where I was least likely to find a moment to eat).

FRIDAY: a sausage roll from a chain bakery in the city centre (my day off, so the chance to indulge in high-salt, grease-laden bliss).

Given that eating while sitting was nothing short of miraculous, the prospect of a lunch with cutlery, a wine list and, perhaps most crucially, no interruptions was a luxury, so when I was invited out to lunch at a restaurant in town by a kindly congregation member, I almost bit their hand off. It is the solemn duty of clergy to enjoy the full glory of creation and that includes lunches. So, on that fine September afternoon, I luxuriated in the three-hour-long glow of this one. There was a soup of passing beauty, a roasted hunk of beef, which managed to be both perfectly charred and perfectly rare, and to finish, glory of glories, a panna cotta. Oh, and several bottles of red wine. Now, I won't quite say it was a rush-of-blood-to-the-head moment, but when I stood up, thanked my host for their kindness and stepped out of the restaurant, the world undoubtedly seemed to be a happier, fuzzier place. Filled with an uncharacteristic affection for the human race, I idled dreamily back towards the church where – I thought – I might conclude this excellent after-noon off with a nap before evensong. As I continued this bucolic train of thought I stepped, lightly but with a determined purpose, directly into the path of an oncoming taxi.

The vehicle screeched to a stop just short of my shins. The driver, justifiably in retrospect, began to remonstrate with the airheaded cretin who had almost rendered him culpable in a homicide (or at least a very slow-motion insurance claim). But as I turned – which happened at a quarter of the speed it should have done, the adrenalin having fought a brief futile battle against the panna-cotta-pudding-wine-and-*petit-fours*-induced lethargy – and began profusely to apologize, something strange happened. Or, rather, given my past experiences of irate taxi drivers, something almost fantastical.

The man caught sight of my collar and a smile spread across his face. The *f* that was forming across his lips transmuted into 'Sorry there, Father', this followed by a making of the sign of the Cross so rapid and practised that it might have qualified as a martial art. I didn't really know what to do – I continued with my apology, then lifted my fingers in a vague benediction by way of thanks at his generosity in apologizing to me for my own idiocy.

Maybe it was because I was so at peace with creation and my place in it that this incident had occurred – a reminder, perhaps, not to settle into such post-prandial existential smugness ever again. All I knew for certain was that it was nothing I as an individual had done that had turned his justified fury into a forgiving smile. Once again, it was the collar. It occurred to me that I was being forgiven on borrowed credit (a concept that we Christians think about rather a lot). Perhaps a priest who had gone before, almost certainly of a different denomination, possibly now dead, had shown this man's parents a kindness during a difficult winter, or had come up with just the right words at a tragic family funeral, had said the right thing in a school assembly or put an anxious bridegroom at his ease. It was that priest he'd seen and forgiven when the collar flashed in front of him, not me.

It dawned on me then that I was standing (or wobbling at this point) on the shoulders of giants. The wander back was concerned not with idle fancies as before, but with meditating on the power of that funny bit of linen – of the trust placed in it and, behind that, lurking in the shadows, the abuses it had enabled. They and their shame are never far from our shared clerical conscience. It was, in short, all rather a lot to take in on a fuzzy autumn afternoon.

3.

Rice Cruspies and Rape Alarms

HARVEST TIME

Despite it being a time of such stuttering awkwardness, the months after ordination – a golden September and October – were, undoubtedly, a time of growth. This wasn't only true for me, of course: this is the time of year when even urban parishes are filled with vegetables grown to positively comic proportions. Everyone remembers the harvest festivals of their youth, that cryptic time of year when children are sent into school with a tin of beans or packet of pasta snugly wedged between the homework and a packed lunch in their rucksacks.

On the one hand, especially in the midst of the concrete and plate glass of a city centre, this feels like a pointless evocation of a synchronized, plentiful rural world that never really was. On the other, for the faithful, it serves as a reminder of creation being under the guidance of God, an important reminder in the age of easily delivered food and cheap, invisible labour. Months of work, unseen by the vast majority of us, go into that which we consume in an instant. For each of us who sits, comfortable and fat, there is another for whom true hunger is still a reality. One of the things the Church should be good at is reminding us of awkward truths. We are used to wandering into a supermarket and being able to buy any type of food at any time of year, yet the UK also has over a million people using food banks (of which a sizeable proportion are Church run).

Precisely how harvest is marked varies enormously. You might think it seems a particularly ridiculous thing to mark in a predominantly urban nation in the midst of the twenty-first century and, at first, I'd have agreed with you. Plenty of churches see it as a vague embarrassment of the calendar. In some places it receives merely a passing mention in prayers, but in others it becomes a jamboree, with hymns referencing long-forgotten agricultural methods, paper plates heaving with miniature pork pies and soapy lumps of cheese and, yes, the largest concentration of amusingly shaped vegetables you'll ever see in a church. Local variations aside, almost everywhere will have some sort of collection – I've been part of collections in Liverpool and London, in parishes without a cow or plough in sight. These are normally initiated with clear instructions – normally a stated preference for long-life and tinned goods, which are then categorized and sent to help feed those in need.*

---

* Possibly the most vicious argument I ever witnessed in a church was centred around just such a categorization procedure. Two ladies the sunnier side of seventy locked

Harvest is also a time to marvel at how unwilling some people are to comply with those clear instructions. For those of us who rejoice in the odd and ephemeral, it's a delight to see the exceptional weirdness of things people bring in. Amid the tins of beans and the spaghetti there are always food items that seem positively deranged in their conception and can only convincingly be explained by the presence of some cartoon maniac in the marketing departments of several major supermarkets. In fact, due to our association with a food bank (which some people clearly misunderstood as a place where you could deposit the oldest or oddest item from your kitchen cupboard), my colleagues and I became obsessed with such packets and tins, texting examples to one another when we found an especially bizarre or patently inedible example in a donation bin. Harvest for me, therefore, was a bit like Halloween.

Our own congregation were inevitably sensible and unfailingly generous in their donations, providing the tinned soups and teabags required to keep a variety of projects going. However, our location in the city centre meant that we were routinely visited in the lead-up to our harvest thanksgiving by an anonymous selection of either maniacs or wholesale grocery buyers gone rogue. These bizarre donations fell into a number of categories:

---

horns – I regret to say voices were raised and personal insults flew – over the question of whether tinned salmon counted as a 'luxury item' or not.

INAPPROPRIATE FOODSTUFFS. When Jesus said, in His parable in Matthew's Gospel, 'I was hungry and you gave me something to eat', I'm fairly sure He did not have in mind a novelty gummy bear the size of an eighteen-month-old child.

RECEPTACLES WHOSE CONTENTS WERE TOTALLY UNIDENTIFIABLE. Tins that appeared to have gone through a sand-blasting process, which had left them corroded and devoid of labelling; chocolate bars presumably bought from the last corner shop before the sun, reducing them to a state no longer recognizable to Newtonian physics; tins with labelling written in an unidentified language and a sell-by date written in a numbering system hitherto unknown in the West – experts in the harvest collection assure me that they almost always contained squid.

FOOD RENDERED INEDIBLE BY THE DONOR. The best example of this was a chocolate birthday cake. Nothing wrong with that, of course, and we ask for some cakes and sweets to ensure that those who are hungry do not have to subsist on a joyless diet of wholewheat pasta and sugar-free beans alone. However, this particular cake was already missing a sizeable chunk. The box had then been crudely resealed with masking tape in a poor attempt to disguise its obvious dismemberment. Handling it felt like the harvest collection

equivalent of body snatching. Another classic of
this genre is the random assortment of foodstuffs
that the donor has thoughtfully collated into their
own pick 'n' mix selection – normally two fistfuls
of loose Bombay mix hurled into a dog-poo bag
and artfully crowned with a single cake bar from a
'Not for Resale' multipack alongside something
perishable (a lemon, a suspiciously soft cucumber,
and once – particularly unpleasantly – some fish).

FOOD RENDERED DUBIOUS BY ITS OWN
BRANDING. While I'm sure that a packet bearing
the legendary 'Rice Cruspies', with hellish
Picasso-like renditions of elves supposed to be
Snap, Crackle and Pop daubed on its side, probably
wouldn't kill anybody (unless, of course, its mascots
were granted the gift of tortured existence by
some malevolent spirit), handing it over to a
family with a face that says, 'This food conforms
to basic standards for human consumption,' is a
challenge. Equally, while I can't claim to be
expert on what is or isn't halal under Islamic law,
I don't think handing a packet of 'hamburger-
flavoured peanuts' (with the only indicator of
their origin being an ominously vague 'Made in
EU' stamped on the back)* to a lady in a hijab
would do wonders for interfaith relations.

---

* It is surely a sensible rule of thumb that the wider the
geographical location of origin, the more dubious the

FOOD THE PROVENANCE OF WHICH WAS
UNCERTAIN. It might have been the case that
Ronald McDonald himself decided to deposit a
catering pack of branded muffins in our harvest
donation box instead of at the branch of the
fast-food restaurant to which they were
addressed, but the impact bruise and engine oil on
the packaging gave them more than a slight air of
'fallen off the back of a lorry'.

All of these are real examples, but such was the level of
donation around harvest time (a testament, to be serious
in the midst of this, to the generosity both of Liverpool
more generally and specifically of our kindly congregation) that the collection developed its own subculture,
and I don't just mean in terms of microbes. It got to the
point where certain items became so difficult to hand out
to people that they acquired their own names and reputa-
tions. There was one particular packet of supermarket
own-brand instant mashed potato we christened 'Grayling' because, like the eponymous cabinet minister of the
2010s, it was always there even though no one wanted to
take responsibility for it. Grayling survived at least two
harvest donation deliveries and subsequent handouts.
    One of the things the clergy promise when they're

---

foodstuff will be. Foods from a specific town or village are
good (Melton Mowbray springs, jelly-encased, to mind);
foods that coyly offer up only a continent or multistate
trading bloc are not.

ordained is to feed God's people. This is primarily through Holy Communion, gathering together varied, vastly disparate individuals to proclaim that 'Though we are many, we are one body because we all share in one bread.' Being fed there, in worship, enables, or rather inspires, that one body to go out and feed those in need (once, of course, they have sifted through the poo bags of Bombay mix and the Grayling mash). So it was that I put to bed my cynicism about harvest's relevance in the modern world, realizing it was a blessing of that which we really need to keep going, namely food and drink. Therefore, harvest became not only a celebration of the continuing miracle of growth in terms of our food and sustenance, but a dawning period of spiritual growth too, a period of realization that the fruits that grow from the root of faith are many and varied.

Flowers are always present around harvest. It is the time of year when bands of doughty and determined flower ladies dress churches in dappled gold and rusted orange, synchronizing their long-planned colour schemes with the high autumnal light that streams through stained-glass windows to create little Edens on window-sills and in ancient niches. And ours were all ladies: when it was suggested by an individual of obsessively progressive outlook that they might be called 'flower women' instead, one redoubtable regular replied, 'Oh, no! Makes us sound like some sort of exotic strip-show troupe.' All, that is, except one.

Just round the corner from the church I served at in Liverpool an imposing hulk of a building was occupied by the Home Office. It was something of a last-chance saloon for people making asylum claims and when, inevitably, some met with the cold stare and folded arms of unsympathetic officialdom, the church became their first port of call and the very last bastion of hope. I would often get a call in my office to say just such a person wanted to speak to a priest, so I spent many hours providing what I hoped were sympathetic words and open arms.

One such asylum seeker from Iraq had wandered into church feeling very low, as low as a person might ever feel. We prayed with him, we put him in contact with accommodation, appropriate medical care and food, yet something was still missing: he wanted a task, a purpose, something practical to take his mind off the labyrinth of law and bureaucracy he was trying to negotiate. As it happened the senior flower lady (our very own Boss of the Buddleias, Don of the Daffodils, Hyacinth Head Honcho) had put in a request for more hands on deck to help with the harvest displays. Could the pairing work? I doubted that growing up in Saddam's Iraq had necessarily involved crafting an angel out of chrysanthemums, so presented the offer to him with several hundred get-out clauses, fully expecting him to seize one. To my surprise, he was game and went along one Friday, travelling on the bus from the forgotten corner of the city to which he had been banished by a bundle of paperwork.

The arrangement was a roaring success, a reminder that official scepticism (in this case my own) is rarely justified, and that the church, at its best, is where relationships that would not happen anywhere else become possible. It was hard not to see it as a blessing – 'God giveth the increase,' as Paul says, in his first letter to the Corinthians. Over those months, I came to learn that much of ministry was sowing a seed, then walking away to allow something holy and good to spring forth. Harvest conspired with grace to teach me a valuable lesson about what really feeds people, and deep respect for the silent magic of the flower room.

The flower room in my church had a mysterious quality. I cannot remember exactly why we were in there in the first place but I knew, on entrance, that something was bound to go wrong. It felt as if the three of us – myself, our parish administrator Jean and the parish assistant Louis – were trespassing into a place where we shouldn't be, like King Uzziah in the Second Book of Chronicles who entered the tabernacle in the Jerusalem temple and got leprosy for his trouble.

Things started off fine. We eased the door open and entered on a respectful tiptoe, in a manner reminiscent of many people on entering a church. Working in a building designated as sacred is a strange experience: the vast majority of visitors come occasionally and reverently, associating the place, rightly, with the immensity of the Divine and with watershed moments of life, love and death. Awe, though, is less easy to replicate when you inhabit that space every day. Never mundane or unaffecting, it becomes familiar. Over time its little quirks of design are recognized, any change in its fabric noticed, its spiky grandeur softened by affection. However, every church has at least one area that is unofficially outside the direct realm of clerical control. In many it is the vestry, where beady-eyed sacristans rule supreme,* ready to chastise any priest who might daub a gold-brocaded vestment with the remnants of their lunch.† In others it is the office or the churchyard or the kitchenette (the Church of England and slum landlords are among the few property owners who believe the instalment of such is of benefit to interior design). In our church, it was the flower room.

Whatever brought us into this *sancta sanctorum*, it involved rifling, and rifle we did, through boxes of wire, tins of ribbon and drawers of secateurs. The flower room was no Hall of Mirrors, and three of us squeezed in there made the search interesting from a logistical viewpoint. Normally – and this perhaps is what gave it its sense of

---

* A sacristan is a lay person whose job is to run the sacristy, where all the gear for the clergy is kept. They serve as part dresser, part carer and part prompt for when the microphones are still on when the clergy are about to swear.

† I am exactly this sort of priest – in fact, I'm a walking stain magnet. My excuse is that it's genetic – I have, and this is the absolute truth, never watched my paternal grandmother complete a whole meal without spilling some of it. Thankfully, I have always been fortunate enough to serve alongside sacristans who have been models of tolerance. The holder of that office in Liverpool, a kindly man devoted to the Church, was doubtless regularly inconvenienced by my ability to attract wax, grease and grime to his beautiful vestments, but he was always far too good a Christian ever to say so.

the sacrosanct – only one person ever entered: the Orchid Overlord, the chief flower lady. Indeed, she worked on her own in there so often, decapitating roses and binding lilies, that the Church Council had seen fit to buy her a rape alarm, in case she ever needed to attract attention when no one else was around. Now, the last thing the three of us wished to do on that fateful day was attract attention to ourselves yet, in a cruel twist of Fate, what should come flying out of an upturned box of floral foam bricks but that very device.

The three of us stopped as, in slow motion, the rape alarm fell to the floor and, on impact, began *very* loudly to do its job.

'WEEW WEEW WEEW . . .'

They say there are five stages of grief. It's not a model I'm normally especially convinced by: in my experience each grieving individual reacts in their own particular way at moments different from anybody else's. I would be prepared to grant, though, that we three went through the classic stages almost simultaneously over the next few minutes as we endeavoured to stop half of central Liverpool coming to our aid.

'WEEW WEEW WEEW . . .'

The screech was so obnoxious that the phase of 'denial' manifested itself as a group lie that this would be easily solved. There was a big button on the front of the device that we pressed in turn, certain – as only a group trying vainly to solve a problem can be – that each of us doing the same thing would have a different effect. I'm told that this is one of the key indicators of insanity. Louis mashed

it first, then proffered it to Jean and me with the shrug of
a man who has discovered that a promising big red button does nothing when pushed.

'Let me have another go,' offered Jean. More button
prodding to no avail.

I cracked my knuckles. If ever there was the moment,
surely, for clerical exceptionalism, this would be it. God's
grace would shine down on me, as it always has. So, with
a clerical flourish, I applied a podgy pink digit to the
button.

'WEEW WEEW WEEW . . .'

'Maybe if I just press *this* bit—'

'WEEW WEEW WEEW . . .'

'Perhaps if I *twist* and press—'

'WEEW WEEW WEEW . . .'

'Or try to—'

'WEEW WEEW WEEW . . .'

'BASTARD!'

I shouldn't like to narrow down *too* precisely when we
shifted from denial to anger but I have a suspicion it
might have been around then.

'WEEW WEEW WEEW . . .'

By this point we had got round to Louis again so I
thrust it back at him. He began the process anew, but
with some creative new flourishes: he threw it to the
floor, picked it up, threw it to the floor again, mashed it
with his fingers, then passed it to Jean, in whose hands it
carried on exactly as before.

'WEEW WEEW WEEW . . .'

'Everything all right in there?' An old man, who'd

46

clearly come into the church for a moment of peace and quiet, popped his head around the door gingerly.

'FINE, THANK YOU!' I lied, slamming the door to the flower room in his face and creating an even more concentrated space for the noise to fire around in – like a karaoke booth or one of those containers/coffins that people get fake tans in, but with more begonias.

'WEEW WEEW WEEW . . .'

We had seemingly exhausted all rational and technical solutions and were becoming increasingly desperate. Then: a brainwave. The flower ladies were keen on creating all sorts of tableaux to exhibit their talents; often this involved straying from the strict definition of flora and introducing other objects – candles, rocks, once a very impressive netting system with what appeared to be a real crab attached – into the proceedings. I picked up a rock. I looked at Louis. I looked at Jean. Should we?

'WEEW WEEW WEEW . . .'

We began smashing our weapons into the alarm with all the glee of chimpanzees that had mastered the use of rudimentary tools.

The door creaked open again and the old man, who was clearly now sufficiently concerned and/or intrigued to risk getting his nose bashed again by the door, peered through the crack with all the tremulous fear of the recent purchaser of a haunted house in a formulaic American film. What met him was the sight of three church staff violently smashing at a small plastic cube. He quickly shut the door, leaving us to work through the 'anger' stage of the process.

'WEEW WEEW WEEW . . .'

'WHY WON'T IT STOP?' This was less a serious question, and more a howl into the void.

'PERHAPS WE COULD HIDE IT.'

Tea and cake were a crucial part of the flower ladies' routine, so alongside the accoutrements of flower arranging sat the paraphernalia for afternoon tea. Pride of place went to a selection of biscuit tins commemorating various royal weddings. They were arrayed for use according to the comparative success of the marriages in the eyes of the flower team (I don't think our Iraqi friend had much of a say in this taxonomy, unless there was a King Farouk shortbread box they kept hidden somewhere). All this occurred prior to the Duke of Sussex's 'divergence of views' with the rest of the family so a box decorated with the grinning visages of Harry and Meghan sat on top of the pile, and within, the remnants of some lemon drizzle cake. I ripped off the lid and hurled the alarm into the tin.

This made things worse: we now had to watch the fixed smiles of the duke and duchess pulsate faintly as the alarm continued its screeching in an even more confined space than before. Logically, we began to smash the tin instead.

Would I have to stay in there until the cursed thing ran out of battery? Would they have to brick us in like a group of adulterous nuns? I paused from my Neanderthal smashing and imagined a future scene:

(Faintly, from behind a wall): '*WEEW WEEW WEEW . . .*'

Tour guide: 'And here is the famous Liverpool Wailing Wall, where you can still just hear the alarm that caused the curate, parish assistant and administrator to be bricked in some forty years ago.'

My internal soliloquy was interrupted by Louis landing another solid bash on the screaming square of plastic – still to no avail. I sighed. It would never end. This, I suppose, was depression, followed swiftly by acceptance. Maybe it would be pleasant to be bricked in. I'm sure the rector would miss us at first but he'd get over it and replace us. After all, Jean and Louis weren't such bad people to spend eternity with. We coped with city-centre sirens and the constant horn blowing of departing ships on the Mersey. Surely we'd get used to the rape alarm after a while.

'WEEW WEEW WEEW . . .'

Suddenly Jean picked it up, her hand narrowly avoiding another blow rained down from above, poked the pin that dangled from the offending object's side into a hitherto unseen hole and, lo, blissful silence reigned. We breathed heavy sighs, and looked at one another with the gaze of relief that protagonists adopt at the end of Hollywood war films. How could we have missed the pin? It came as no surprise to learn, in retrospect, that the alarm had the same mechanism as a hand grenade.

We turned our backs on the chaos of what had once been the carefully ordered flower room and wandered past a group of lunching office workers at the entrance to the church. The old man from earlier was whispering to them in a style that distinctly said 'witness statement'. I turned to my colleagues: 'I think we just about got away with that.'

It might well have been the tagline for those early months, when the awkward and the holy seemed to be dancing in sync.

4.

Exorcizing General Franco

'Oh when the saints, go marching in!
Oh when the saints go marching in!
Oh Lord I want to be in that number,
When the saints go marching in!'

It is a soggy day in late October, approaching All Saints'
Day, and the above – one of the better-known spirituals
to have come out of the Deep South – is being bellowed
(well, more whined) by a group of sodden students on a
rugby touchline deep in the Home Counties. It wasn't
enormously convincing. I was back, just as the year turns
auburn and grey, at my university college for an old
members' rugby match, in which increasingly paunchy
accountants and hospital consultants chase nimbler current students and their long-lost glory days in muddy
frustration.

My college had been St John's (as in the Baptist, patron

saint of builders, hail, spasms, and Penzance), which had teamed up with a college dedicated to St Anne (patron of equestrians, second-hand-clothes dealers, grandmothers and Canada) to field a joint team that was known, by compromise, as 'The Saints'. These saints were a group of student rugby players (the respective patrons of students and rugby players being St Thomas Aquinas and the suitably butch St Sebastian respectively), who were the subject of this half-hearted fanfare, and my equally limp applause, as they marched, or limped, back to the pavilion at the end of the game, muddied and bloodied, courtesy of early middle age.

Later, as I sat watching the rain, on the train out of Oxford, my mind (addled by the gins Ian, the college groundsman, had so generously provided to those he liked on the touchline) turned to sainthood. We still talk about saints – 'She has the patience of a saint', 'He's no saint' (although some in the Church like to talk about 'heroes of the faith' instead),* but what exactly do we expect of a saint? Do we even know any more? Are clergy supposed to be saintly? Or are we just human? As is often the case on trains, my mind turned inward – never a good change of direction, bringing out an uglier side to my nature (the patron saint of the ugly is, of course, St Drogo). Would a saint have taken quite as much joy from

---

* We talk about secular heroes even more, so what was intended to make things sound less 'churchy' and weird actually makes them sound even more bizarre. I think even the most dyed-in-the-wool non-believer understands what a saint is.

those grubbier tackles? Would a saint have accepted a fourth gin? Would a saint, as I did later on, jump the barriers to avoid paying 20p for a wazz at Euston?

In truth, as and when the actual saints *do* go marching in, they will be just as motley a crew. There will be plenty of limpers – from St Servatius (a bishop who travelled so much around Europe that he acquired the patronage of foot troubles) to St Margaret of Castello (a medieval nun who had one leg an inch and a half shorter than the other). There'd be plenty of bleeders too – from St Veronica (who dabbed the bloodied face of Christ) to St Januarius (a bishop who was originally condemned to be eaten by wild beasts but then had his sentence commuted to being beheaded in a volcanic crater when the critters proved not too peckish for bishop burger that day. His dried blood is kept in a vial in Naples and liquefies on important anniversaries to much rejoicing.)* And plenty with weird injuries that would put any rugby damage to shame.

This is before we get on to their personalities. Pity the poor saint who has to march next to the kleptomaniac St Juniper or the notoriously gloomy St Luke the Younger, who used to sleep in a trench to remind himself of death. In fact, the longer one studies the saints the more it becomes clear what a weird, wonderful and often gloriously annoying bunch they are. Given that – and bearing

---

* Perhaps the most influential medical saint from Naples (just to keep things to a nice, broad category) isn't Januarius but St Aspren, a Neapolitan convert from the first century whose prayers were asked for help with headaches and who, of course, was the inspiration for the brand name Aspirin.

in mind this is an assembly that includes St Arnulf of
Metz, who cured a plague by telling his congregation to
drink alcohol instead of water – I decided that the fourth
gin would easily be forgiven. As for that stolen wazz at
Euston, I could have asked for the prayers of either St
Vitalis of Assisi (a hermit who'd led a dissipated and
drunken existence as a youth – seems appropriate) or
of the wonderfully named St Henry the Exuberant,
both of whom have somehow found themselves as
patrons of pee.

Autumn is the period of the year when the Church
thinks most about this bedraggled holy grouping. Indeed
a whole day is dedicated to them: the feast of All Saints
takes place on 1 November, which fell only a week or so
after my dash back to university to watch the rugby. As
such, there was a seasonal appropriateness to that dirgeful
singing in a muddy field.

As my train finally drew back into long, dark Liverpool
Lime Street station, I felt thankful to be surrounded by, as
the Bible calls them, 'so great a cloud of witnesses'. Few
groups can link the campfires of the Deep South, a soggy
rugby pitch in Oxford and a vision of the open gates of
the Heavenly City, but the ragtag bunch of martyred,
munificent, matronly or just plain maniacal people we call
saints managed it, at least in my head, that afternoon.

Over the following week the nagging question from
the train remained on my mind. As I spent the next few
days preparing suitably gory costumes and stories about
the saints for our Sunday School to celebrate the great
feast, I wondered what makes for saintliness in the

twenty-first century. There aren't many opportunities for the restoring to health of lepers (St Francis) or being cut in half by a big saw (St Simon Zelotes) going round the parishes of England these days. In terms of personal development, thinking about saints can often lead clergy to feel they're not cut out for the job. My tendency to measure myself against the successes of people I knew at theological college or university was bad enough, let alone also having to work out where my microscopic achievements stood against ridding a whole island of snakes (St Patrick), turning bathwater into beer (St Brigit) or carrying my own head for six miles after it was lopped off as punishment for being a Christian (St Denis).

Contrary to popular belief, martyrdom isn't the only way saints gain their saintliness. As the contemporary usage of 'saint' suggests, many went around being bastions of charity, kindness or self-sacrifice. While those are all qualities a vicar might be more likely to aspire to than martyrdom, it's worth owning the frustration that accompanies many little acts of charity.

This is not to say that works of charity and mercy are not the delight of the Christian calling as well as its duty. Far from it. But there is a particular obligation when one is wandering around dressed as a *professional*. Put another way, people might not expect a vicar to be a saint in the miracle-performing sense, but they certainly don't expect them to go around being a blatant sinner either.* It is also

---

* Of course, there are plenty of environments in which a cleric might find themselves judged as guilty before being

not to say that clergy are invariably paragons of self-giving virtue – often the opposite. (A wise priest once told me that 'God ordains those he cannot save by any other means.') Experience (and my own love of stubbornness) tells me that the English are so well versed in their grudge-bearing that they would happily imperil their own eternal salvation because they once observed a vicar fail to open a door for a pensioner. We're all moral hypocrites at heart. It's just that those of us who are ordained are foolish enough to advertise the fact.

In the back of my mind there were stories of the saints who found themselves being nice or helpful to a person who appeared to be someone they'd normally ignore (like the beggar who received St Martin's cloak, or the child St Christopher helped to cross a river, earning them the patronage of tailors and travellers respectively) but turned out to be a manifestation of Christ.* Consequently, you feel as if your possible saintliness is under constant examination, like your charity is permanently

proved innocent. Just before they ordain clergy, bishops are meant to give a 'charge', a profound and moving reflection on the responsibilities of the life as a priest that awaits them. One bishop, some years ago, was famous for dispensing with that and simply giving his new clerics one piece of advice: 'Never enter a public lavatory while wearing a dog collar.'

* St Martin also managed to earn himself the title of patron saint of geese after a flock gave away his hiding place while he was trying to escape from some people who, rather irritatingly, wanted to make him a bishop. Imagine that, having your life ruined by some aggressive waterfowl, then having to spend the rest of eternity praying for them.

on parade. Even if at the other end of your interrupted journey lies some greater act of virtue, the love of your life or a pot of gold, you are obliged to stop and deal with whatever quibble or query is thrust in front of you by a member of the public who might be – as the Letter to the Hebrews reminds us – an angel or even Jesus in (a very convincing) disguise.

One such example occurred, as these run-ins often do, on a railway platform. As a non-driver, I was being punished by the whims of the post-Dr Beeching Furies and having to change trains for the second time in the depths of suburban Liverpool. On the face of it the journey was indisputably one of charity – taking Holy Communion, as the church did every month, to bungalows, retirement homes and smart semis whose inhabitants, due to sicknesses of mind or body, spent long weeks alone and housebound. On this particular round trip through the further reaches of Merseyside I was accompanied by Louis, our parish assistant, an expert in resurrecting conversations as they circled round the same topic for the fifteenth time as, on occasion, would happen.

It was one of those days when rain or heat or goblins had rendered the British Rail service even less reliable than usual so we found ourselves waiting for half an hour on a long platform, past which faster, less goblin-afflicted trains would fly at great speed. Lured by the need to get a ticket for this next leg of our complex journey and by the potential of a vending machine – there is no better mid-journey respite than a Diet Coke and some Monster Munch – we made our way to the peeling yellow-painted cabin that served as a ticket office and waiting room.

I purchased Louis's and my tickets from a bastion of long-faced indifference who sat, masticating loudly, behind a glass screen. There was only one other figure in the ticket office: an elderly lady, bent over a large bag in which she was rooting for something, accompanying herself with noises that implied she wasn't having much success. It was hardly an act that will guarantee me a place among the assembly of the saints but, given I was there as an ambassador for the one who told us 'Whatsoever ye would that men should do to you, do ye even so to them', I had little choice. Louis and I gave one another a knowing nod and I went over.

'Do you need some help?'

'Oh, thank you.' It was a sweet, lilting American tone. 'I've been trying to get a taxi but I can't find my purse with all my European money.'

Normally entering a railway station as a pensioner and asking two young men to fish around in your bag with the hope of retrieving a purse would be asking for trouble but, as I've said before, a clerical collar has a great moralizing effect on the person wearing it. I handed the bag to Louis, who held it open for me to rifle through. Eventually a purse was produced and handed to our grateful American friend.

'Now, I just need to work out which ones the machine will take.'

Late millennial that I am, I had foolishly assumed she was looking for cash to pay an already booked taxi driver and had ignored the presence of an ancient pay phone in the corner of the station room. This was clearly going to be a longer process than I'd initially anticipated.

The concept of angels in disguise flashed through my brain. Who was supposed to be the angel here? Me? A cynical newly minted clergyman, who still struggled to feel full of zeal and love for God or my fellow man or anybody else at any time before 10 a.m.? It seemed unlikely, and while my good deed was undoubtedly motivated by faith rather than a happy-go-lucky altruism, it seemed pretty clear that the saint in this – or, frankly, any – situation wasn't me. Could it be this lady in front of me, who appeared to be visiting south Liverpool from some time in the 1970s? Time travel is the sort of thing an angel in disguise would get up to. After all, the Seven Holy Sleepers of Ephesus miraculously fell asleep in a cave, then woke up and wandered about three centuries later, all to escape persecution by a Roman emperor. All well and good, I thought, but would a saint or angel or even Christ in disguise *really* choose the Edgehill interchange for a moment to test the faith of the newest of the shepherds? Surely they had bigger fish to fry.*

My happy fantasies of being asleep for three hundred years were dashed against the rock of reality by a gleeful transatlantic cry: 'I think I got one!'

She held out a coin that, even from a distance, I could tell was not British legal tender. It was huge, a dull, worn

---

*   About five thousand of them, to be exact.

gold colour, and bore a face I didn't immediately recognize but was certain could not be Elizabeth II's on account of the moustache. 'May I?' I picked it up to examine it and found myself eye to beady eye with none other than, as the writing round the coin's edge proclaimed, FRANCISCO FRANCO CAUDILLO DE ESPANA. While this damaged the possible claims to hidden sainthood (Jesus sent off the disciples specifically telling them not to carry purse or shoes, and *definitely* didn't tell them to try to pay using coinage bearing the image of the Fascist dictator of Spain), I have to say there was something rather sweet, and indefatigably American, about this lady. She was certain she could still use the currency picked up from her last trip to continental Europe, which had then barely recovered from the Second World War.

'I'm afraid that won't work. You see, that's General Franco.'

'It's who?'

'General Franco. He used to run Spain.'

A blank look.

'FRANCO.' I cranked up the volume impatiently. Definitely not saintly – not least because there's already a patron saint of loud noises: St John Macias.*

'Oh.' She dropped the coin back into the aged purse with disappointment, as if it were an error on the part of

---

* He used to ride around Lima on a donkey asking for donations for the poor. When people didn't cough up, the donkey would stand and bray at its highest volume until they did. Definitely a strategy to add to any future parish fundraising effort.

the Mersey Rail network that they didn't accept long outdated, Fascist coinage. She rooted around again. 'How 'bout this one?'

I squinted at the image held between the two wrinkly digits. Franco again.

The question of how she had come into possession of what appeared to be the entire currency reserve of Falangist Spain flashed across my mind. By now I would happily have shoved my life savings into the pay phone (a total, I should add, that would have given her a good two minutes' worth of phone time, max.), but all I could feel after a quick and undignified root around in my trouser pockets were the notes I'd been given as change earlier and a stick of gum.

I looked across the ticket hall for help. The world's least enthusiastic railway employee had clearly heard our conversation and was surely in possession of enough coinage to give us change, presumably at least *some* of which would be legal tender outside 1950s Madrid. Unfortunately, all that emanated from behind the glass was bovine chewing. No joy there.

Suddenly I realized that, despite the scene, we were in the twenty-first century. I hadn't fallen into a timeslip. Phones, taxi apps and automated payment: all these things *did* exist. Take that, Franco. I weighed up explaining the concept of Uber but thought better of it and simply told her a taxi would be coming soon, which it duly did, the cavalry in this situation. We saw her into the vehicle, waved her off, and here endeth the lesson. Or so we thought.

'Oh, shit,' said Louis, glancing down to his side. 'I've still got her bag.'

Clearly things hadn't descended quite far enough into farce. Cue the two of us hurtling up the slope, waving, as the taxi driver transported our new friend/merrily unaware victim of mugging to her destination. Thankfully, the gremlins affecting the railway network that day had turned their attention to road traffic: far from careering off into the sunset, the taxi had ground to an ignominious halt at what I'm sure proved to be the first red light of many.

Louis and I banged on the windows of the halted taxi and he handed over the bag to its grateful owner. 'Oh,' she said, 'you're an *angel*.' No, I thought, but after all that I bloody well hope you are.

We rushed back to the station to find our train just pulling away from the platform. No good deed goes unpunished, eh? It was only the next day when I noticed that the callow figure behind the ticket desk had inadvertently given me twenty instead of ten pounds' change when I'd bought the tickets. And they say virtue is its own reward.

The episode reminded me of all the reasons why I wasn't a saint. I had only entered into an act of charity under severe duress, I'd found the experience a near constant round of frustration and in the end I'd inadvertently swindled a railway company out of a tenner. Hardly grounds for canonization. But the point of the saints is that they were human too. The feast of All Saints isn't about reciting the tales of superheroes of the faith.

Rather it's about reminding people that all of us are better off trying to tread a path of sanctification, trying to love our neighbour, no matter how consistently irritating they may be and no matter how often we slip up while trying to do so.

Of course, run-of-the-mill vocations are about much more than just being nice – indeed, a cursory look at a platform like Twitter will show you that those who proclaim their niceness loudest are the real masters of profound nastiness. Besides, it seems to me that niceness is all too often a device of suppression: 'Be NICE' is the refrain bellowed at the child to stop them edging over into chaos. But if Christianity is about living in a way that reflects the idea that humans are in receipt of undeserved and unlimited love and grace, there must be an element of joy in our lives. Joy can be loving and caring, of course, but it can also be cheeky or subversive. The saints were rarely nice in the conventional sense – but they were bringers of light and of joy.

There are almost as many ways to refer to the saints, as a grouping, as there are saints. While many of the specifics of saintliness beyond the generically nice aren't known today, they remain a part of popular culture in at least one particularly mystical way. One, now rarely used, Old English term for the saints is hallows, which, of course, gives its name to Halloween, a corruption of All Hallows' Eve, the day before – you guessed it – All Saints' Day. That might seem a weird mismatch, to think about ghouls and ghosts at a time when we're meant to focus on the super-holy but when it comes to blood and gore the

lives and deaths of the saints rival any Halloween theme.*
In fact, given how weird and wonderful the saints are, I
suppose it's no bad thing to make a fuss of them at this
time of the year when even the secular world is attuned
to the weird.

And attuned to the weird – no, not just weird, but
supernatural – it still certainly is. Regrettably, the link
between the Church and the world of the occult is
mostly, these days, in movie form. The film *The Exorcist*
has much to answer for when it gets to late October. I
shall never forget when a chaplain of an Oxbridge college came to visit me and made the mistake of ducking
into a pub on the way for what he thought was a quiet
pint. This strapping rower turned cleric was subjected to
what was, in essence, a prolonged groping by a hen party,
who absolutely refused to believe that he wasn't a stripper. The poor man lost a cassock button in the process.
October in Cambridge might be a suitable time and place
for a man in long black robes to sit unnoticed in a corner
of some ancient inn but in Liverpool it was generally –
and not unfairly – assumed you were on your way to the
Horny Halloween Bottomless Brunch.

That said, there are still occasions when the clergy
brush up against the world of the occult. Belief in evil
remains very real for a very large number of people, and

---

* I would say Halloween costumes could 'eat their hearts out',
but that would seem a little insensitive to St Ignatius of
Antioch who actually did have his heart eaten out of him by
lions.

not all of them can quite bring themselves to believe that evil can be explained away as an accident of nature or as something that proceeds from humanity. Rather, there remains an instinct to blame it on the supernatural. For all our supposed rationality, there is still much to be scared of in many people's minds.

The form these fears can take will vary. Much of the time people describe medical phenomena that doctors have assured them simply are not there. Failing to find a medical solution, they come to a priest, crediting dark powers or supernatural attacks as being responsible for anything from tinnitus or corns to serious illnesses or even impending death. A willingness to listen, no matter how far-fetched the issue may seem, saying a prayer with the sufferer, allowing them to feel safe in church, is often enough to make these attacks go away. Sometimes all people want is someone to take them seriously. People's houses also prove to be focal points of potential activity. I am asked to bless houses and flats all the time. Sometimes people feel uncomfortable in a new place or something changes in one that they've known for some time, and they feel unable to explain it in normal ways.

This even happened in my own lodgings around this time of year. I got a call at about 11 p.m. from Crispin, my training incumbent – a.k.a. the unfortunate organ grinder designated with making me a passable monkey. There were two flats linked to our church and the inhabitants of the other were complaining of some strange noise: could I investigate and see if it was an intruder? I can't say I'd noticed any sounds but I'd been eating crisps and watching *Jackass 3* at full volume so I was hardly the most efficacious night-watchman. I went into the church and then the hall next door, above which lay their flat. Nothing. I reported this accordingly and returned to watching Americans dive into lakes of poo.

Half an hour later, another call. Could I check again? Might it be something else? I began to wonder whether I should go and pray, perhaps bless some holy water, sprinkle it around. Should I consider saying Holy Communion? Wave a crucifix about? I wasn't planning to squat shivering and smelling of garlic in the middle of a chalk circle, but I felt the tenants probably expected *something* from a priest. I went down again, mumbling the Lord's Prayer as I went. After closer inspection of the far end of the hall, I was confronted with the full horror of the culprit: a famously recalcitrant radiator that somebody had left on.

Being involved in any of this might sound a bit bonkers to you. I'd like to say it's all part of the rich tapestry of faith but, in truth, very often these occult situations seem as weird to the clergy as they would to the man in the street. I know of one priest who was asked to go and pray at a house suspected of being haunted and then, to add to the creepiness factor, received two children's drawings through the post by way of thanks. Another forgot to bring holy water and conducted a house blessing using some hastily blessed gin he'd brought along for a party afterwards.

Yet, as unusual as it may all seem in the twenty-first century, the Church of England still keeps, in every diocese – the chunk of the country under a particular bishop – a diocesan exorcist. These days they call them 'diocesan deliverance ministers', which makes them sound like the sort of person who'd leave you a 'We're sorry we missed you' slip after knocking on your door with all the force of a gnat. 'We tried to deliver your exorcism at [ILLEGIBLY SCRAWLED TIME] but sadly you were out. Please come to [INCONVENIENT ADDRESS] between [HOURS YOU COULDN'T CONCEIVABLY MAKE] to have your devil/demon cast out.'

In fact, they're highly trained and experienced clergy, who either have degrees in psychiatry or act only in accordance with a psychiatrist to whom all instances of paranormal activity that seem to go beyond the explicable are referred. I can bless a house or check a dodgy radiator, but I'm sure there will come a time when I'm dealing with stuff way beyond my pay grade. In short, there are millions of things I don't know about or understand, and I'm happy to add the world of the supernatural to that list, where it can sit snugly alongside 'how to properly poach an egg' and 'the exact pronunciation of Reykjavik'. I've not yet had a brush with the supernatural that I couldn't explain via a dodgy heating system or the plentiful malice of humanity but I thank God for the professionals being on hand if it does happen. It's part of the Church's job to be there for you in every sense – whether it's a genuine malefaction by the powers of darkness or just your taps.

In that season of Halloween, of saints and ghouls, as

the nights drew longer and physical darkness became more present, I suppose I began to feel a sense of how it might be that I and the Church more widely were called to shine in the darkness of a world that often doesn't care, doesn't notice or doesn't believe. Part of this entails shining a light into my own soul, my own irritations, my own shortcomings. This responsibility isn't just about being available, a man in a funny outfit who can't say no to requests for long conversations, or help with a taxi, or advice about plumbing: it's about being a bringer of light, and a light that isn't just our own sparkle or force but something bigger than ourselves. Not just human, but a glimpse of the Divine.

Tough gig.

Yet shining a light in the darkness can take many forms, whether it just means poking a torch into a loft or being the only person to listen to someone whose world seems permanently dark. Neither act is superhuman. As the saints themselves show, aspiring to be saintly can be married to being human. Indeed, what are the saints if not fallible humans made good? They may have done that in marvellous, almost mystical ways, or quiet, humble, ordinary ways. Both, I suppose, are ways of shining lights in the midst of the world's darkness. That's ultimately who the saints are: shiners of light.*

---

* Although the specific patron of lighthouse keepers is St Venerius the Hermit, let's not downplay his achievements.

5.

Falling in Line?

I grew up in a military family. Until my mother banished them to an outbuilding – because they were, and I quote, 'fucking horrible' – parts of my family home were filled with prints of fierce-looking military men, often painted midway through some sort of exercise or parade. On family holidays I was taken to places like Stirling Castle, to back rooms of dusty regimental museums to gaze on brocade-trimmed faces, all with the same notable lack of facial structure and hangdog glare that I saw in the mirror. Right the way back to Waterloo or thereabout, Butler-Gallies, including my own father, put on military uniform as actual soldiers, not like the people who spend their weekends pretending it's the Battle of Edgehill.

It shaped my childhood in a number of ways, although my father had left behind any relationship with the armed forces when I was young. Having spent so much time in an ordered environment like the army, I think he found

much of the lack of structure related to having five children too much to bear. He would fly into brief, intense
and futile rages at the chaos and idiocy with which
he was surrounded. There were all sorts of spurs to
these – my siblings throwing a cat into the tub while he
was trying to enjoy a bath, my grandmother's constant
fly-tipping in his garden, or when he put the handle of
the sitting-room door on the wrong way round and spent
an afternoon in enforced solitary confinement until my
mother returned home and let him out. These furies
were never directed at individuals but rather at the universe. It was all quite theological, really.

They say that temper is hereditary, but I vowed very
early on that I would, instead, be part of the world of
chaos rather than a futile force of order, so I joined, for
reasons I hope this book makes clear, the Church of England. I expected my father to be sceptical. When you've
been shot at in a very real situation it probably makes
having someone daintily tripping around in linen and
lace talking of peace and goodwill a little bit annoying.
In fact, he was pretty supportive. He and my mother,
being good, progressive Generation X parents, had
decided to tell all five of their children that they would
be proud of them 'no matter what' they ended up doing.
I sincerely doubt they had in mind 'become a C of E
vicar' when they dispensed that bohemian advice, but
once the words had been uttered it was hard to go back
on them. It did at least cushion the blow when my sister
departed for an artists' commune a year or so later.

When I told my father that I wanted to be ordained,

he merely gazed at me with a well-worn hereditary
hangdog look and remarked: 'In many ways it's not so
different from the army. The outfit's stupid and the pay's
crap. Carry on.' My mother, I'm sure, might easily have
said the same of her profession in the National Health
Service, but I think they let them wear what they like
these days.

Yet I don't think we escape our inheritance as easily as
all that. Some people might see a clerical calling as an act
of rebellion against a bloodstained history. They'd be
wrong. I don't deny that Jesus is the Prince of Peace. The
bits about 'turning the other cheek' are some of the most
popular parts of the Gospel although it is to be observed
they tend to be quoted by those keen on doing some face-
slapping. In reality my father's observation wasn't so
facetious after all, despite the seeming differences between
those hard-nosed military men of action and the effete
elderly vicars that lurk in the popular imagination. Doing
the job that appears the opposite of the one your parents
did doesn't mean you escape those ghosts – especially not
when you find yourself in an institution as bound up with
the life of the nation as the Church. I've probably spent
more time dealing with military and civic affairs than I
would have done at a more obviously swashbuckling
job – like arms dealing or accountancy.

How so? Well, the C of E remains the established
Church in England and so, at those moments when this
famously introverted nation throws stereotypes to the
wind and decides to indulge in a bit of community
togetherness it still, very often, looks to the Church for

some sort of guidance and organization. Crispin, for instance, was constantly on call to advise on events as diverse as a wine-tasting showcase organized by the city of Bordeaux to the exact order of civic dignitaries at a funeral. Now, given how chaotic some parts of Church life can be, you may think that's a bit like asking the National Federation of Pissheads to run the open day at the brewery. However, it's one of those odd anomalies of recent Church trends that civic occasions are better attended than they used to be. Perhaps when it comes to organizing public rituals the clergy know what they're talking about.

At these markers in the calendar of national life, people are quite willing, happy even, to come to church. It's trying to entice them in on the third Sunday in August that can be like pulling teeth. *C'est la vie* – but it's a quirk of modern Britain that Remembrance Sunday is now one of the busiest days in the Church's calendar. In some places only Christmas is busier. When I first joined the Church I naively hoped that November would be a nice lull before the madness of Christmas,* but the middle chunk of November is a period of considerable crossover between military, civic and clerical activity. As you can see, my attempt to escape my military past has gone swimmingly.

---

* Only once did I manage a holiday in November, just after the frenetic week or so around Remembrance. I decided to take a relaxing escape to stay with my sister in Beirut, which promptly launched into an attempted revolution the day after I arrived.

By all rules, this shouldn't be so. Around the time I was born, as the twenty-first century loomed, there was a sense that Remembrance Sunday would die out soon. The veterans of the world wars were getting older and fewer, and nostalgia was out of fashion. Surely we were looking forward to a brave new century of progress: what had a few doddery old men in berets and blazers to contribute to that?

Fast forward the nearly thirty years of my lifetime and I was standing in a set of municipal gardens where the great and the good – councillors, clergy, MPs, even the local celebrity who'd been brought in to sing a medley of songs at the end of the event – were giving way, in hushed, respectful silence, to the progress of a wheel-chair, a fragile, rattling thing that stuttered its way past these famous figures. In it was a veteran of Arnhem, the infamous 'bridge too far' where the 1st Airborne Div-ision lost nearly three-quarters of their strength while fighting against overwhelming odds. He had seen friends, barely older than boys, die in front of him. He had been involved in the struggle against perhaps the most notori-ously evil regime in history and had willingly jumped out of a plane on to a continent under the grip of Nazism to bring about its end. He was old now, of course, and gripped the wreath he was to lay with wizened hands. As he placed it, with help, at the foot of the modest slab of granite, he saluted and a tear fell down the contours of his face. It was hard not to be moved.

This was no glorification of violence but a marking of sacrifice, loss, the passing of time. With themes like that, you can see why the Church is involved in such events. It's perfectly understandable that, for most people, these are themes they might want to dwell on just once a year, but given their central role in the Christian story, vicars have to think and speak about them more like once a week. Of course, civic life is not always as moving or appropriate as it is in Remembrance-tide. The weird role of the Church of England as the national Church involves being roped into all sorts of civic events. I have seen or been directly involved in: a service of blessing, which transpired to be a four-course lunch, on board the Cunard cruise liner the *Queen Victoria*; a memorial service for the Duke of Rutland's pony; a sprinkling of holy water on a new knife-disposal bin; and a service for a new lavatory facility, which ended with a celebratory first flush at the final 'Amen'. Some people think the Church shouldn't be involved in such things, particularly Remembrance because it amounts to 'baptizing violence'– yet the Church is still involved, busy blessing wreaths and WCs across the land.

Despite, or perhaps because of, continued involvement with such events, by November of my first year I thought I had largely got used to the being a cleric in public thing. I'd got over the collar. I'd stored up some witty ripostes to catcalls, and I'd honed the off-the-cuff sermon. I'd worked out small-talk with local councillors, military officers, service users, service abusers, local dignitaries, people pretending to be local dignitaries,* minor

---

* Perhaps the best of these was the man at a dockside event who claimed to be the managing director of a major

royals, and even, *even*, fellow clergy. Remembrance season was full steam ahead. Clerical duties delivered with utmost efficiency, no undue moping or superfluous dwelling on my own thoughts allowed or, frankly, possible. In some ways, the busyness of that specific part of November helped. While October gave long hours to dwell on saintliness and my own unholy failings, the period around Armistice Day meant I was trying to cram six Remembrance services into one weekend, making it pretty tricky to dwell on the wrongs or rights of being there. I just got on and did it.

In fact we had almost reached a clinical approach to such things. With a two-minute silence at 11 a.m. on the dot as the centrepiece of any service, timings had to be perfectly calculated. Indeed, the handler of my early clerical years, the ever-patient Crispin, had passed on to me exactly how long various psalms or prayers would take to fill in various chunks of time before 11 a.m. when, inevitably, a civic dignitary who said they'd talk for ten minutes actually talked for two. We thought we'd had it down to a fine art. Of course, as Proverbs 16:18 reminds us, 'Pride cometh before a fall.'

Some churches – in bucolic corners of the countryside, often with a single simple war memorial – have just one simple, dignified service. In some ways, rural public

---

shipping line. 'You see that boat?' he said, pointing to a huge cruise ship with P&O emblazoned on the side, the famous Peninsular & Oriental. I nodded. 'Well, I own it. I'm the "P".'

life is still much more in tune with the rhythms of the Church year. Harvest has a more tangible meaning when surrounded by fields than it does among the concrete; the gathering round the war memorial is something a whole village might do, where a whole city could not. But, necessarily, fewer big events go on in the country-side than in a city or town. By contrast, having served all of my ministry in city centres, I am used to multiple services, multiple memorials and multiple opportunities for things to go wrong. In Liverpool alone we played host to memorials to the fallen of the Corn Traders, the Accountancy Guild, the King's Liverpool Regiment, about fifteen of His Majesty's Ships, and the entire Merchant Navy. It was the latter memorial service that provided the corrective to my being puffed up after a paltry five months in the job – for what else is ministry but a constant cycle of getting too big for your boots and being cut down to size?

The Merchant Navy Remembrance service was always fraught with difficulty. First, it required the skill of being in two places at once (back to those saints again) as it happened across two locations, starting at church and ending at the memorial, a short walk down to the edge of the river Mersey. Invariably, a hardy few – mostly people who had been coming to the event since before I was born – would get this wrong each year, arriving at church while we were at the memorial or going to the memorial, then glaring at those of us who had come from church at the appointed time as if we were seeking to mark this solemn occasion by putting on a procession

of centaurs wearing nipple tassels. Second, the Mersey is
not one of the world's calmest rivers: if Strauss had tried
to trace its movements in music and written 'The Beautiful Grey Mersey' instead of the 'The Beautiful Blue
Danube' it would have ended up sounding like an acid-
house mix. She is, it goes without saying, feisty in
mid-November.

Things initially went to plan. There was some wind
and the Mersey was high as she always is at this time of
year, with waves licking just underneath the balus-
trades, but it hardly seemed appropriate to call off an
event honouring those who had kept the country sup-
plied in *all* weathers because of a bit of spray. Anyway,
I'd received heavier soakings courtesy of people eating
with their mouths open at civic buffets. I was standing
with my back to the river, facing a motley crew of veterans, supporters and tourists trying to work out
whether this was a live re-enactment of *Sgt. Pepper's
Lonely Hearts Club Band* or not. It was strange, looking
out on the sallied ranks of these wrinkled, uniformed
men. The devil was working well that day and I felt a
wholly unwarranted puff in my chest, imagining I had
followed all those ancestors, and was there in a military
tunic rather than a cassock, wondering whether I had
gone into the wrong job after all. I cast what I suppose
I thought was an officer's eye over my troop. In fact,
even though I would do most of the talking, I was the
least important person there. Next to me was a naval
dignitary, whose importance was demonstrated by a
jacket so covered with metal that it would have given a

security scanner a nervous breakdown just thinking about it, and, the most important person present, the bugler.

The bugler was important for two reasons: one, the constant need for me to mark time was obviated by the presence of someone with a loud brass instrument. Put simply, the silence started when she played and ended when she played. The second reason was that, until recently and after negotiations between the Merchant Navy and the rector, the music at the service was provided by an amateur sea-shanty group. I want it on record that in the unlikely event that I die in the service of my country, under no circumstances do I want the anniversary of my sacrifice to be marked with a rendition of 'What Shall We Do With A Drunken Sailor?'. These well-meaning gentlemen agreed to step aside only when a professional bugler was suggested. Consequently, I was much more grateful than I might usually have been for the presence of a piercing-sound emitter directly next to my ear.

In fact, sea shanties scrapped, and grumbling about bi-location largely suppressed, things were going well. An elderly gentleman did burst forth from the crowd, with the enthusiasm of a confident greyhound making a false start, and tried to lay his wreath during the health-and-safety/welcome announcement at the start, but that aside I was already chalking this up as a win when the Last Post began to play. The two minutes passed and, as we were coming to the moment when Reveille would sound, a sudden gust of wind from behind hoicked up my cassock and the skirt of the bugler and, in a moment of perfect synchronicity, lashed a wave of spray from the river in our direction. The result was that we received an impromptu and ill-directed enema, courtesy of one of Britain's dirtier rivers. The naval dignitary was, on this occasion, wearing trousers, so escaped with the comparative dignity of just looking like he'd pissed himself. Flustered, the bugler and I corrected ourselves and Reveille was played – though, of course, the two minutes' silence had ended moments before, the audience roaring with laughter at this gross infringement of clerical dignity.

As I made my way, damply, back to the church, I reflected again on the Church as bringer of joy and chaos. It's all too easy to think of those we remember in November as unsmiling monoliths·in sepia, easier still to think of those veterans who remain as frail and occasionally frustrating old men, but they are human, and it's testimony about their humanity that provides the most moving moments of that week in November. Frail hands, single tears, eruptions of the giggles: all very human. The image of soldiers – our image of the past – is so often based on superheroes and war films, which often feel very far from a recognizably human reality, deliberately so. Remembrance services provide a humanizing touch to all that. Perhaps the best form of remembrance is to continue with the stupid jokes and inappropriate laughter that inevitably will have comforted others in much darker times. And if a vicar getting his skirt blown up and his pants splashed is what it takes to do that, then so be it. Perhaps I, perpetual class clown, wasn't in the wrong job after all.

†

While November is, of course, busiest with Remembrance events, it seemed that year to gather a glut of other civic and military events, as if the great and the good saw it as their 'church month' and thought they might as well fold all of their services and commemorations into a three-week period. So it was that I found myself marking the shift from autumn to winter, from being truly new-minted to being part of the furniture, surrounded, very often, by the only people in British public life with an outfit stupider than mine: mayors.

I've met more mayors than you can shake a heavily lacquered, gold-embossed stick at. There are different types, of course: you've got your classic mayor, an ordinary councillor who has been selected by lot to spend a year opening new bus shelters while dressed, inexplicably, as a Tudor. Then there are your next-level mayors: local power-brokers you've never heard of but who technically have the authority to knock your house down and would probably do so were it not beyond them even to coordinate bin collection days. Then there are kingpin mayors, who run conglomerated regions with made-up names and budgets the size of small South American countries. Everything is under their jurisdiction but, crucially, nothing is their fault. The power of a mayor is in inverse proportion to the extravagance of their outfit and their likelihood of turning up to civic events. Your classic mayor would turn up to the opening of a crisp packet, while your mega mayor would come only if the BBC were shooting a specific documentary on crisp packets, allowing for some media exposure, or if the crisp packet had made a considerable donation to the mega mayor's party. When you've hovered awkwardly around enough post-event bunfights, you learn to recognize each type on sight.

Of course, city life isn't just about buffets, gold chains and fake ermine. It's also a world in which people suffer from homelessness, drug addiction and road rage. The Church is just about the only place where those worlds can and do collide. Sometimes this can be moving – I recall one civic procession in which the elected politicians, who had just spent an hour or so giving speeches about solidarity and care for the poor, breezed past a young homeless woman shivering in the November wind. It was the group of clergy who stopped, acknowledged her, sat down and talked.

Unfortunately, being in the no man's land of public life doesn't always result in such touching opportunities for prophetic care of the poor. Often the place at which the different sides of a city – the carefully managed public face and the chaotic reality of urban life – collide is the scene of shouting, swearing and, on one particular occasion, shit. I forget which civic service was involved, only that it coincided with a long-running dispute between the church and one of those people who make up the 'other' face of the city.

Tasha often slept in a doorway just around the corner from the church. Her waking hours were spent insulting passers-by, her favourite lines being 'Big nose', 'Nasty bastard', 'Fat paedo', which, as I tried to explain to her on several occasions, was probably why they were often reluctant to give her money. We did what we could for her in church, letting her raid the food-bank donation box for biscuits, making her tea (milk, fifteen sugars) and letting her use the loos under the parish office.

It was the last of these privileges that resulted in the dispute. Three days in a row, the disabled loo had been caked in wet toilet paper, little flecks spattered all over the walls, like the scene of some sort of horrific papier-mâché-related crime. While Tasha denied it was her, it seemed unlikely that the other regular user of the lavatories, one of our elderly servers, was responsible. Sue, our church cleaner, had had enough so that morning, when Tasha came in for her ablutions, I told her firmly that she'd need to use the public facilities from now on. Apparently this made me 'an arsehole'.

Now, preparations were well under way for the civic service and, apart from the run-in with Tasha, things were going well. There was one minor complication: Jean, our administrator, had finally convinced the rector to have a new carpet laid as part of the redecoration of the parish centre. This meant that before passing through the office, anyone – whether they were clergy, from the AA group or the lord lieutenancy – had to go through an elaborate shoe-scrubbing ritual to preserve the immaculate shag pile. If Our Lord Himself had returned that very morning, I would wager that He would have been required to give His sandals a wipe before entering. That aside, all was prepared. The orders of service were printed, I had my cleanest cassock on and Roger, our faithful verger, was busying himself getting the church in order for the arrival of the civic dignitaries.

What was that Bible verse again? Pride cometh before a fall? I was so pleased with how things were going that I had snuck into the rector's office, settled down at the desk and begun to trawl absent-mindedly through Twitter. Everything was under control, God was in his Heaven and all was right with the world. It was then that I heard a clarion cry that will cut through my consciousness until my dying day: 'There's a shit in the church! Roger! The carpet!' Jean's cry was futile. Roger had already broken through the carefully constructed cleaning station and was already smearing what later proved to be Tasha's dirty protest into the carpet, having dragged it through from the choir stalls to the office on his right shoe. All the while, as traumatized people often do, he simply repeated, again and again, 'There's a shit in the church!'

Of course, it was no longer accurate to say that it was just in the church. It was now in the office, the hallway and on Roger. I bolted out from the rector's office, hoping against hope that I would find the situation wasn't as bad as it sounded. Wrong. What I found instead was Roger backing out of the door to continue his unfortunate muck-spreading operation just as the service was about to begin.

He continued his panicked progress as the assembled civic dignitaries of Merseyside began to arrive. Bechained mayors and mayoresses were met with the sight of a positively carnival-like procession: at the front, Roger, dancing a sort of boogie-woogie shuffle as he scuffed shoe polish and poo along the flagstones, followed by Sue, pouring hastily diluted bleach behind him as he went. After her came Jean who, as the epitome of professionalism, forgot about her carpet, and instead delicately placed a mound of tissue over each area where Roger had contrived to leave a skid mark. And at the end of it all, as a walking metaphor for clerical impotence, me.

Eventually we caught up with Roger, procured a change of shoes, identified and cleaned the original site of the dirty protest (second pew from the back in the choir stalls: the connoisseur's choice). The service went ahead. It was a much stranger celebration of the ups and downs of city life than was originally intended but, I think, not inauthentic. Although everything did smell of bleach. And shite.

†

I suppose when I told my father I was joining the Church all those years before, I thought I was doing something quite counter-cultural. But if the season of Remembrance and the world of religion in the public sphere have taught me anything, it was that there is still a great hunger for rituals, events or even a theology that binds people together in marking things we think are important. There's still a sense of sacrifices that should be valued and service that should be marked. Sometimes the Church can think it's now too small or should be too holy to step into certain spaces. But whether it's the civic space of the mayors and mayoresses, or that of the less fortunate or, God forbid, an attempt to build a space between the two, it's still something we can and should do. Perhaps it isn't so counter-cultural, and perhaps my calling wasn't so different from the sense of service that inspired those flabby-faced ancestors of mine. The chance to be at that point where the holy meets the worldly, the chaotic meets the ordered, not just in November but all year round was, as I was reminded, one of the reasons why I'd felt called to priesthood in the first place. Strange that it took a crap in a church and an involuntary Mersey enema to remind me of that but, to quote the well-known dictum, 'God works in mysterious ways, his wonders to perform.'

6.

Strap-ons and the Apocalypse

Advent calendars were never a great success in my child-hood home. Five children, each with the attention span of a concussed goldfish, were never going to be drawn to the idea of waiting to eat one chocolate per day each over the course of twenty-four days. In fact, the sooner the whole Advent charade was over and the inevitable gorging happened, the bigger your winnings would be. If, for instance, you waited until, say, the early hours of 20 December to creep downstairs and stuff yourself with the remaining treats designated for you and your siblings, you'd bag a measly thirty mini-chocolates, two handfuls at most, to be hoofed into your face like they were cocaine or a hip flask of Windolene.

However, if, like a pre-adolescent Sun Tzu, you adhered to the maxim that 'Opportunities multiply as they are seized', you crept downstairs after bedtime on 30 November, you'd be the possessor of 120 crude chocolate approximations of parcels, snowflakes, fir trees and other things totally unrelated to the Nativity of Jesus Christ. Of course, such a raid had its recriminations, but carefully strewn wrappers and shredded calendars could easily suggest to a casual observer that this was the fault of the dog. It rarely worked. Normally it resulted in tears before breakfast and the entire family called to the scene of the crime for a Poirot-level interrogation. The culprit would be outed, performative moaning and belly-clutching often being the tell-tale clues that gave them away. Soon enough our parents gave up on chocolate and started to replace our confectionary-filled Advent calendars with pictorial ones, each door containing a twee scene of Victorian winterdom, all equally unrelated to the Nativity of Jesus Christ.

All of this was a disappointment – a disappointment that even now couldn't be soothed by a spot of low-grade chocolate thievery.* When invited to play at the houses of other children, I would look with envy at mantelpieces groaning under the weight of lazily branded cardboard and cheap chocolate, which I'd been denied because of hereditary impatience. In my pre-Christian days, before I felt there might be something bigger, that perhaps there was truth in the words of Jesus Christ, Advent struck me as a particularly crap part of the year. After all, who likes waiting? I am the sort of person who has missed key early plot points in almost every film I

---

*   The low grade here refers to both the thievery and to the quality of the chocolate.

have ever seen in a cinema because I refuse to wait through the adverts. Waiting for Christmas – one of the best things about childhood – seemed to me the most frustrating, pointless thing of all.

Fast forward twenty-odd years. It is the start of December and I'm frustrated again by waiting. After an uneasy truce post Poo-gate, some members of our homeless community have been allowed to use the toilet again. I'm told by a departing Louis that someone is in there but is taking her time. I am due to lock up the church but she's still in there. Basic respect for dignity means I don't want to burst into a ladies' loo, like an LA cop doing a drugs bust. So all I could do was wait.

As I stood, a resentful lavatory sentry, I could hear the sounds of pre-office-party revellers gathering on the city streets outside. Advent, I reflected, is *meant* to be about waiting, about the in-between time, about now but not yet. It's not a very popular concept, in an age of instant gratification. The idea that anything, from a bolognese sauce to a first kiss, might be better after you've waited a while for them is never going to be popular when you can stroll round the back of the bins at Tesco, right now, and instantly get hold of both. It seems a bit of a cop-out to blame that childhood impatience on zeitgeist rather than a mercurial lust for cheap chocolate but I think growing up in a world that had decided even a phone call was too arduous a way to order a pizza and replaced it with a few taps on a screen probably had some small effect on my attention span. In the case of the occupied loo, I knocked loudly and poked my head round the door.

Empty. I had been waiting without any point, waiting for the sake of waiting. With Advent, though, the waiting – and what we gain from it – is *exactly* the point.

Advent is the time of year associated with the apocalypse, the end of the world. In a certain way this makes sense, especially when you consider how impatient most of us are. Indeed, such is the tendency of the human mind to look ahead that Christians have been trying to fast forward to the Second Coming of Christ for almost as long as they've been thinking about the first. Advent was historically a time when clergy would preach about the 'Four Last Things': death, judgment, Heaven and Hell. Unsurprisingly, the Church doesn't bang on too much about them during Advent. Imagine the festive scene:

'Ah, a knock at the door! I do hope it's carol singers. "Jingle Bells" is my favourite.'

'Hello, madam, have you heard the one about an unending lake of fire?'

That said, I think we should keep one eye on the apocalyptic at this time of the year. The temptation to be cheerful, generous and well fed for the entirety of December not only takes the shine off Christmas, which becomes one long hangover, but it's not really possible for some people. I found that for a lot of people December really was a truly miserable time, replete with less than jovial ghosts of Christmases past. 'Jingle Bells' really does make some people think of torment. Lots of quiet tears are shed among the tinsel. Having a period of the year that says, as Advent is supposed to, 'This is a bit crap, but something better is coming,' is actually more hopeful a message for those people than unending smiling. Despite my nature, I tried that first year to keep alive a sense of the waiting, a sense of the apocalyptic, amid the holly and the fairy lights. The little slogan I would repeat to myself during this season of the in-between, adapted from those traditional practices, was 'Watch and wait, fast and pray.' Watch for signs of goodness and mercy, wait for the coming of something better, fast from excess so you'll enjoy it more when it comes, and pray for those in need. I didn't always succeed in this pious aim – I still don't some years later – but that first ordained Advent still felt like I'd come a long way from depriving my siblings of 120 poorly moulded chocolate Santa heads.

There's another reason why I feel particularly attuned to the historic themes of Advent – of time passing and contemplation of mortality. It's also when my birthday falls, the twelfth, if you're interested. Not many illustrious birthday buddies for me, I'm afraid: Clementine Churchill, Frank Sinatra, and an Australian serial killer known as 'The Brownout Strangler'. In fact, for all my pious desire to focus on those ancient Advent themes I had to spend my entire birthday locked in back-to-back carol services, giving Christmas blessings and singing Christmas songs a full two weeks before the event. Now, I know I said I hated waiting but there are limits. Whatever your views on the exact historicity of 25 December as a birthdate for Christ,* singing

---

* I say 'whatever your views' but do draw the line at the idea that Christmas is actually a bargain-basement version of a

God rest ye merry, gentlemen, let nothing you dismay
For Jesus Christ our Saviour was born upon this day . . .

on the day that had given the world 'The Brownout Strangler' seemed in poor taste, not very Adventy, and, crucially, not top of the list of presents I'd asked for to mark turning twenty-seven.

However, the event was closer to the principles of Advent than it looked, despite the music choices (and, believe me, given we were doing requests, 'God Rest Ye Merry, Gentlemen' was nowhere near the most theologically dubious song).* It was a carol service specifically designed for those who probably wouldn't get an invite to any other carol services. While the doctors, lawyers, police, bankers, fire brigade, estate agents and amateur learners of Spanish all had their own dedicated carol service, the people who aimlessly wandered the centre of town on a wet Thursday afternoon didn't. They just watched and waited.

So it was that we clergy and musicians did our own watching for everyone to turn up. And turn up they did, a mixed band, from stressed office workers to pensioners, hospital and care-home patients to nursing mothers. It soon became clear that the clergy – Crispin, the eternally

---

   repackaged pagan festival called 'Saturnalia', mostly because it's historically and theologically utter, utter balls.

* People were meant to stick to the approved list of carols on the sheet, but that didn't prevent one lady from unsuccessfully requesting 'Do Ya Think I'm Sexy?' by Rod Stewart.

charitable Bill, one of the assistant priests at the parish church, and me – would be acting as entertainers as much as clergy. We prayed, of course, and read the age-old story to the assembled, but we had to do so in outfits even more dubious than our usual gear.

The allocation of costumes had been awarded to a younger member of the congregation.

'You can be a Santa!' I was told, and had a hat thrust in my direction.

'Watch and wait,' I said, in my head. 'Fast and pray.' I accepted the hat with a smile. It could have been worse: Louis had to be an elf.

Things were ticking along well. Or so I thought until I saw Crispin having a quiet word with the bandmaster while I was preoccupied with trying to call a raffle and give a vaguely coherent explanation of how God the Father and God the Son were different *and* the same to a man who'd washed his complimentary mince pie down with a glug of super-strength cider.

No sooner had I finished my rambling and borderline heretical description of consubstantiality than the band struck up the only tune I dreaded more than 'Frosty The Snowman'. The low, unmistakable moan of an unenthusiastic crowd being made to sing 'Happy Birthday' to someone they'd never met filled the church. It was sweet, in its own way, but at the front, I longed for the Four Last Things to occur there and then. Or at least for a swig of the super-strength cider. Strange, I thought then, for a clergyman to be embarrassed by that sort of attention, given we pop up in robes and invoke the living God every Sunday.

I got through it all with a magnanimous wave – think ailing Soviet premier greeting a tractor parade. Then, after a much more enthusiastic singing of 'We Wish You A Merry Christmas' (12 December!), I made my way to the back of the church to shake hands and say goodbye as we shuffled people off into the darkening afternoon.

I prepared a sickly Christmassy smile for the first customer. I got a question in return. 'So, how old are you, then?' This was not with the emphasis on the 'you' (as if it were being cooed over a babe in arms) but on the 'then' (as if it was being barked at a new arrival in Alcatraz).

'I'm twenty-seven,' I replied, maintaining the diabetes-inducing grin.

'You don't look it.'

'Oh, thank you, something of a baby face, I suppose, and I've been—' I was cut off mid-fawn.

'I'd have said mid-thirties.'

What was most galling was that this person, though seemingly alien to any concept of conventional politeness, apparently had an eye for an ill-maintained skin regime and was, frankly, probably right. I responded using the autopilot phrase every cleric uses in December: 'Do have a *lovely* Christmas when it comes.'*

---

* It really is a catch-all phrase to avoid answering any question directly at that time of year: Q (at the church door): 'What was that sermon all about?' A: 'About having a lovely Christmas when it comes.' Q (in the barber's chair): 'Any plans for the break?' A: 'I suppose I'll try and have a lovely Christmas when it comes.' Q (on a motorway hard shoulder): 'And do you have *any* idea how fast you were

STRAP-ONS AND THE APOCALYPSE

Would I have any luck with the next candidate in the line-up?

'Ooo, born on the twelfth day of Christmas! Lucky you!'

My eyebrow twitched. 'Don't say it,' I said to myself. And then said it: 'Aha! It's not actually the twelfth day of Christmas!' I'd intended this to come out in a tone that implied touch-and-go playfulness, but it emerged in a way that said, 'Menacing *and* anal.'

'Yes, it is.' When it came to menacing and anal, I was clearly going to get as good as I gave.

'Well, you see, Christmas Day is actually the first day and after that—'

'No. First of December, that's partridge in a pear tree. Second of December, that's turtle doves.' She began to demonstrate the numbering using an outstretched hand.

'Yes, I know the order. It's just—'

'Third is the hens. French ones.'

'Do have a lovely Christmas when it comes!' I decided to address myself to the swarm of people who were now simply pushing past her, having seen and heard exactly which direction things were going in. Was she going to shout, 'FIVE *GOOOLD* RINGS,' at me? And insist they should be doled out on 5 December?

Fortunately she'd lost interest at four calling birds and gave me a cheery wave as she went off. 'It's all there,' she said. 'Check your Advent calendar.'

---

driving?' A: 'Have a lovely Christmas when it comes.' OK: it's a catch-*most* phrase.

Ah, yes, I thought, the curse of Advent strikes again. I went up to my flat, poured myself a birthday brandy and switched off my phone. That was enough watching and waiting for one day.

Of course, all of these attempts to keep Advent holy made me – and every other cleric who still tries to inject those bits of waiting and apocalypse into the long lead-up to Christmas – feel a bit of a fish out of water. It was bad enough that I spent my period of morning prayer getting into a meditative and penitential zone only then to have to don a Santa hat and 'jingle' at appropriate moments, but I also had the whole social pressure of the Christmas build-up as well. I would tell myself on 1 December every year that I would at least spend my evenings in quiet anticipation, only for my meditative silence to be broken with invites to Christmas parties and drinks. This started long before we'd even reached 'Five gold rings' in that lady's back-to-front twelve days. It's very hard to maintain an air of repentance and reflection on the passing away of the old and the imminent coming of the transformatively new while someone shoves a fifth mince pie into your mouth, and harder still on your fifth mulled wine.

But that first Advent taught me that operating in what feels like a different time zone, according to different rules, is part and parcel of what the clergy are called to. The clergy's experience of Advent is wholly, and neces-sarily, different from that of the public, which, when you work with the public, can be a little jarring. Everyone else is preparing for some time off and throwing them-selves into drinks and parties, and you're stuck using the one bit of free time you have off from photocopying carol sheets having to meditate on the apocalypse. But, like everything, it's a balance. There's taking a consciously different approach from the rest of the world, and then there's just being a smug killjoy. Either way people are going to think you're weird, but embracing that weirdness makes more sense than spitting tacks about what the laity are up to. Sometimes this sense of being different was a gift, a chance to reflect on the role I was now six months into. Sometimes it was simply funny.

People definitely do behave strangely around clergy. There's a sense, I suppose, that we might be carefully placed moles for the Divine, ready at any moment to report any minor misdeed to the Almighty. This is especially true in the lead-up to Christmas, as if we might have access to some sort of grown-up equivalent of the naughty list. When people aren't emboldened by drink – which by mid-December is rarely – a certain sheepishness creeps into their interactions with clergy. I recall being at the ticket barriers at a railway station when a young guy in front of me couldn't get his pass to work.

'Fuck, fucking, fuck,' he proffered, towards the gates, before turning round and seeing me. 'Er, I mean, um, shit.'

I quite liked the idea that downgrading his profanity by one order of rudeness would be enough to let him off whatever Divine hook he thought he might be on.* I

---

* I don't know about you but I have a very clear and defined sense of the order of profanity, both in terms of satisfaction of use and of wider offensiveness. I would list it here but I

didn't tell him that, in his situation, I would probably have reached still further into the pick-'n'-mix of English profanity.

It was on a packed train in the deep midwinter when I was most conscious of this sense of being out of step. I was on my way back from a hospital on the outskirts of the city, having visited someone who almost certainly wouldn't be home for Christmas, and my fellow passengers were there to get into town and snap up some bargain presents. I confess I'd made sure I'd positioned my scarf to conceal my dog collar. It was rather a nice cashmere one – I looked like a very camp undertaker, but it did the job: I wasn't outed as a solemn Advent observer in the midst of a commercial Christmas scene. The mood was tetchy, rivalries for bargains already being formed via steely glares across the busy carriage. I felt a bit as if I was in the complimentary shuttle to the Thunderdome. In fact, it's probably true that the only place in which the secular world now honours the apocalyptic side of Advent is a department store five minutes before closing on any day in the final shopping week before Christmas.

I was idly dreaming, probably of something profoundly inappropriate, when I, and the rest of the carriage, became aware of an altercation happening over my shoulder. A woman had spotted a couple with whom

---

suspect that my bishop will at least want to claim he's read this book, and I shouldn't like to embarrass him at future occasions if people were to ask him whether he'd read the footnote about why 'piss' is better than 'crap'.

she had some history, the exact nature of which we were not blessed with knowing, but it was clearly a negative enough experience for her to refer to one half of them as 'that slapper'. She went on to speculate about the kind of things they might get up to in the privacy of their own home in clear hearing of the forty or so people trundling towards the city centre. This caused equal measures of delight and horror as she catalogued an array of sexual practices that would have left even the most broad-minded cleric a little flushed.*

'Just ignore her,' the object of her abuse announced, in a stage whisper. That was easier said than done.

As we approached the next station the woman began to jostle through the crowd towards where the couple and I were standing. There was a tangible bristle as people wondered whether things were about to take a more serious and physical turn. In fact, she was simply getting off at the upcoming stop. After she had done so, with the train doors still open, she turned back towards the train and pronounced her final sentence of doom: 'And I bet she does you with a strap-on and all.' And with that, our very own pornographic prophetess was gone.

Obviously this got a few laughs, but mostly, as we trundled along towards the next stop on the line into town, there was a whispered dissection of the events. My

---

* That said, it is worth noting that the Church of England's own teaching document on sex, 'Issues in Human Sexuality', includes a sub-section on the comparative virtues of same-sex nipple play.

stop was the penultimate one, where I changed to a different branch. As I made my way to the doors, my carefully placed scarf slipped, revealing my dog collar to the woman who'd been the target of the strap-on speculation.

'Hey! He's a priest! If I'd known that, I'd have slapped her when she said "strap-on".'

I assured her that this valiant display of chivalry wouldn't have been necessary, exited the train to watch and then, for the first time in my self-imposed Advent gloom, absolutely pissed myself laughing.

I spent much of my first ordained Advent watching my own language, carefully trying to preserve the holiness of the season, not wishing a merry Christmas to anybody before the big day, looking suitably penitential in shops, acting as a Twelve Days correction vigilante. As Christmas Eve loomed, though, I realized that was probably a bit useless. That was perhaps the most important lesson of Advent. There is no point in attempting to stem the tide of tinsel. Just as I'd learned when I opened the door to the empty loo, sometimes my active efforts were useless. All I could do for myself was watch and wait, fast and pray. It was oddly liberating. By embracing the uselessness, the being a fish out of water, the being out of step, I was able to laugh and to appreciate the strange holiness of the time I was in, as I did while I watched and waited for that connecting train.

That's the other lesson of Advent, I suppose: that a lot of being a priest is about the waiting, whether that's outside a crematorium or a sacristy or on a railway platform.

Or outside a toilet door. After all, our waiting is not in vain, but with the certain hope that something better and bigger is on its way. That's not just Advent: that's Christianity. As they say, good things come to those who wait. That's not to say that learning to wait, watch and pray, instead of shout and do, was something that came easily, but then it's not meant to. In the meantime, we might as well try to be a comforting Advent presence, watching and waiting for signs of the holy in a world of strap-ons and complimentary mince pies.

7.

Endless Bloody Carols

CHRISTMAS

Advent was nearly over, and things hadn't got any more normal. I'd just watched a man with a big green curtain draped around him climb into the pulpit and start speaking Hungarian. He wasn't the only one in that particular get-up: there was a church full of men draped in green curtains. When you spend most of your week wearing what is, to put no finer point on it, a heavy woollen dress, it's rather nice *not* to be the strangest-dressed person in a room. We were now less than a week away from the big day, what a friend calls 'The Christian Superbowl'. We were also into the final lap of carol services and this one was for a little-known Hungarian chivalric order, whose robes were a rich, deep green. My social media feeds were filled with friends returning to parental homesteads, jetting off in search of winter sun, or simply settling into a solid week of booze consumption in shared houses. I, in contrast, was about to shake hands with a parade of people who looked like they'd taken a tumble in the Wizard of Oz's box room. This was my Christmas now, and I wasn't in Kansas any more.

Just before the gathering of the big-green-curtain men, we'd had the semi-nude fire-fighters. We really did save the best until last. It was actually the annual Fire Brigade carols and, to be fair, I don't think they'd *meant* their Christmas carol service to be a *Full Monty* tribute but it had rather turned out that way. While the performance at the end of the service certainly wasn't the full hen-do experience at 5 p.m. on a chilly afternoon in December – I'm not sure the church heating was conducive to the removal of intimate items of clothing – the desire to include the Fire Brigade Dance Troupe in the annual carol service had resulted in a somewhat saucier ending than we usually had. Put it this way: were I in demand to create a dance routine seemingly constructed around finding an opportunity to flaunt my bulging pectorals,* I don't think I would have chosen 'O Little Town Of Bethlehem' as my backing track. Some members of the congregation were one crotch thrust away from throwing their knickers into the sanctuary. Hardly the vibe you want during 'The Holly And The Ivy', especially as the next line is 'when they are both full grown'.

And so, to paraphrase John Lennon, this was Christmas: a parade of strange encounters, all in the name of making known the joyful message of the Nativity. Christmas Eve was given over to our 'Crib Service', in

---

* A *very* far-fetched counter-factual, I grant you.

which a gang of children, already high on those grand chocolate finales of their Advent calendars, helped put up the crib scene. It was exactly as chaotic as it sounds. It didn't help that our Nativity characters appeared to have been designed by someone who would have been better employed as a set designer at the Moulin Rouge or props master for one of *those* Italian arthouse films. First, one of the shepherds appeared to be doing something absolutely unspeakable, and certainly, for an audience of children, inexplicable, to a frozen turkey. I was assured this was, for some reason, a set of bagpipes, but I remain unconvinced. Second, when you arranged the Three Wise Men in a line − a natural instinct you'd have thought − they appeared to be making passes at each other. I think these were intended to be vaguely Oriental poses (think 'Walk Like An Egyptian') but in fact it looked like an outbreak of mass groping. In the end we managed a relatively un-smutty tableau, although I think an ox and/or ass may have lost its head in the process. As Midnight Mass loomed, I realized I was beginning to flag.

I don't think you can actually be martyred by an excess of Christmas events but by the late afternoon of 24 December I estimated that I had sung 'Away In A Manger' and 'Hark! The Herald Angels Sing' in excess of fifty times. Or, at least, it felt like it as I tried to crank my voice up to bellow the final chorus.* I'd heard the

---

* Different carols, of course, require different volumes and different levels of enthusiasm. I think 'In The Bleak Midwinter' can be sung in a dirge-like, low tone. The

story of the little donkey and Mary and Joseph and the shepherds and the Wise Men more times than was healthy. Could it really be that this, the greatest story ever told, was wearing thin? It wasn't so much that I was annoyed at being 'in the office' over Christmas. I'd spent my childhood with a medical mother and a military father so I was used to the idea of a working Christmas, and Yuletides spent on the battlefield or in the ICU are undoubtedly tougher than those spent on the pointy end of a Christingle orange. It was more that by the time I reached Christmas I was a bit sick – sick from excess of mincemeat and mulled wine, sick from the ceaseless smiling, sick of the endless bloody carols.

†

Every cleric has stories of the madness that is Christmas. It's part of the upside-down existence that we have to lead. Just as the rest of the world is focusing on 'Driving Home For Christmas', the clergy are in church what seems like 24/7. As the congregation gets misty-eyed at

---

oppressive jollity of 'God Rest Ye Merry, Gentlemen' requires you to sing in the manner of a portly, red-faced Victorian from a Christmas card. 'O Come, All Ye Faithful' demands a frantic crescendo, which once resulted in the carol being banned during my time at school after, on the final 'O COME LET US ADORE HIM', somebody got carried away and launched a Book of Common Prayer across the central aisle of the chapel, resulting in a spectacularly bloody nose.

'Silent Night', the clergy are often taking part in loud discussions with drunken revellers that make hostage negotiations look like a spa weekend. As others ponder 'Peace on Earth, goodwill towards men', most of us are one jingled bell away from a multiple homicide. That isn't a moan as such, just another example of how, even at the one time of the year when church-going is considered comparatively normal, we still find ourselves out on a limb. For many people it really is 'the most wonderful time of the year' but they're mostly safely ensconced at home with family and imminent indigestion while we're locking up in the cold. Part of ordination is about not being like other people, but it's at times like Christmas when the reality of what that looks like really bites.

It can't really be surprising that most vicars affect to dislike – or even hate – Christmas. They might hide this behind claims that 'It's got too commercialized' or complaints about the 'once a yearers' who merrily ignore the message of Jesus Christ for 364 days and then suddenly, perhaps overcome by the smoke from those chestnuts roasting on an open fire, get religion and decide they want a dose of the mysteries of the faith. Providing, of course, that it doesn't take any longer than fifty-five minutes.

After my first festive baptism of fire, I came to the conclusion that clerical Grinchiness is largely a result of the sort of timetables described above, rather than great otherworldliness. It's easier to affect a lofty disdain for the whole commercial charade than to admit you're too busy clearing up after curtain-wearing knights, semi-nude firefighters and beheaded donkeys to have that Christmas drink with a friend or relative. Also, to be honest, while my inner curmudgeon wants to agree with such Scrooge-like dismissal of the modern festive season, I'm not sure the Church of England can afford to be quite so fussy. It's an interesting aside that, while numbers for Sunday congregations have been heading south quicker than a swallow with soon-to-expire air miles, the number of people who attend a church service at Christmas time has been growing for the last decade or so. I know of some churches that rely on the Christmas collection plate to see them through the inevitable boiler malfunctions and congregational drop-off of January, when the temperature and general atmosphere inside some churches is closer to the Arctic Circle than the Heavenly Jerusalem. Those people who pop in once a year are better off doing that than never darkening the door.

Here I have a confession to make: I was a 'once a yearer'.* Christmas was the sole moment that religion really did play a part in my upbringing. A bit part, admittedly, like those random porters or soldiers who barge into Act III of a Shakespeare play, impart some incredibly important news, then promptly bugger off again. As I imagine is the case for most children, the knottier aspects of the theology of the incarnation were a little above my pay grade, but I knew about the Baby Jesus and Mary and Joseph in pretty comprehensive narrative terms. I also knew, more selfishly, about the presents it all entailed and so, despite not having any real faith to

---

* Try saying that with a mouthful of brandy butter.

speak of at that point, I kept schtum and went along with it all.

I was in a Nativity play, of course. A straw poll at my theological college found that almost everyone training to be a vicar had played a 'good' part in their Nativity play. I was surrounded by former Marys, Josephs and Angels Gabriel. I, by contrast, had been assigned the part of the innkeeper, the man who'd famously refused to find space for Mary and Joseph, resulting in them having to introduce God Incarnate to the world in an outbuilding. After a lengthy period of delving into the complexities of the character, I'd decided to play him as a sort of Basil Fawlty figure, a man driven to distraction by the frustrations of ordinary life so completely (and arguably understandably) oblivious to the imminent arrival of the Son of God at the back of his digs. It was a performance much admired by critics at the time, but I still couldn't help feeling a little less holy than all those who'd been picked to play the key characters.

Still, it could have been worse: I had a friend at theological college who revealed that he'd been selected to play King Herod. Then again, he *hated* children. Forget horoscopes or the Myers Briggs system, I think the great personality test is 'Who were you in your primary school Nativity?'

It wasn't only school where God crept in during late December. As with many people, Christmas was the one time my family went to church in a year. Unless somebody died, in which case we might deign to go twice. Initially our dose of religion was the Christingle service, the modern tradition whereby the tale of universal salvation is told via the medium of an orange, raisins, cocktail sticks and some dolly mixtures. The combination of naked flames and sharp objects proved too tempting for the destructive side of the Butler-Gallie nature so, as soon as bedtimes allowed, we began instead to attend Midnight Mass.

This was where I first encountered the messier side of the Church. I recall one year we were coming to the end of the service at around the same time as the village pub's somewhat elastic chucking-out time. The little church in the centre of that settlement was of a more relaxed tradition than the ones I have served in, so the service ended not with a solemn pontifical blessing, but with a rendition of 'We Wish You A Merry Christmas'.

Just as the organ was about to strike up this jolly finale, a fully refreshed gentleman wandered in, with the gait of a legless sailor trying to navigate a force-ten gale that has had the misfortune to strike just after he's received, and consumed, his monthly rum ration. Churches are, of course, places of welcome, so even had the sweet ladies on the door been inclined to tell him festively to piss off (as the landlord at the George and Dragon had clearly done moments earlier) they would have been in contravention of Christ's instruction to welcome the stranger. Christ said nothing about strangers who've had a county's share of ale, but I think that would be quibbling. Either way, this gentleman was optimistically furnished with an order of service and invited to sit at the back. Some valiant, last remaining consciousness in the Alamo of his brain heard the opening bars of 'We Wish You A Merry Christmas' and he resolved to join in with gusto. Unfortunately, this last bit of willpower had previously been holding out against the rest of the body's understandable desire to get rid of the volume of alcohol consumed over the course of Christmas Eve. Consequently, his rendition of that family favourite went something like this:

We wish you a Merry Christ-bleurk
We wish you a bleurk bleurk Christmas
Bleurk bleurk bleurk Merry Christmas
And a bleuurrkkkk-ew Year.

Each 'bleurk' had resulted in a comparatively small eruption of vomit but by the time he'd struggled through the first verse, he was standing over quite the pool. He looked down into it forlornly, an abstracted version of his night staring back, like a pissed-up Narcissus. He tried to continue, hoping, by some sort of Christmas miracle, that he might be able to redeem himself and belt out the final line unperturbed by the gymnastics of his own oesophagus. Alas, it was not to be. He managed 'Good tidings we bring', only for a physical expression of those good tidings to make itself known with a resounding splat on the marble floor. By this point people were beginning to notice and turn round, not so much in judgement but in curiosity at what *precisely* the scent was that now so noticeably mingled with those of Christmas tree and incense.

Eventually, faced with the cricked necks of the

TOUCHING CLOTH

congregation and his internal spasms, he gave up. His roaring was no more, and he satisfied himself with the occasional dribble down his front during the final departing procession. Even so, as he staggered out, head held low, the vicar still smiled, shook the hand that was proffered with more than an iota of shame and wished him a very merry Christmas. Quite how he could have got much merrier without being declared medically dead, I don't know, but it's the thought that counts.

Ever since then I've always had a sense that anything could happen during that thin time between Christmas Eve and Christmas Day. I've grown to love the lingering sense of chaos that hovers over a Midnight Mass: there's a sense that it's a gathering of the people of God uncensored; Church After Dark. Then again, nobody's been sick in my church. Yet.

All that said, as a child I often viewed these Yuletide brushes with late-night religion as a sort of penance to be endured before I could enjoy our own family orgy of consumption that I knew would come the next morning,* the one day of the year when it was acceptable to breakfast on chocolate alone. My mother had (indeed still has) absolutely no concept of portion control so we invariably celebrated the birth of the babe of Bethlehem with a

---

* I'm aware that 'family orgy' is an unfortunate run of syllables for a clergyman to write, but not only does this genuinely refer to brandy butter but I'm also conscious that plenty of ordained people have scribbled worse. I recall one cleric, in Norfolk, I think, who had a successful sideline in erotic fiction.

mass outbreak of indigestion. Even in my secular child-hood mind, a trip to church the night before stuffing ourselves stupid was probably the least we could do for the real birthday boy.

I can't say I thought much about the Baby Jesus when I went to those Midnight Masses. I spent most of my time looking round the congregation, even the sober, non-vomiting ones. I would fix my eyes on perfect strangers, in the faintly haunted way that only children under the age of thirteen can, and wonder how they would be spending their Christmases. I would create fantastical, often slander-ous, stories in my head about what they'd eat, what presents they'd receive and how, most importantly, they planned to spend the dead time of Christmas afternoon.

In my search for things to occupy my brain, the one person whose Christmas plans it had never occurred to me to wonder about was the vicar. Now, in my first year of ministry, I didn't have to create a lurid narrative. I was living it. Of course, the reality proved much more banal than I could ever have imagined. I can tell you very simply what clergy do in the rare downtime of any after-noon in December: sleep. Present-buying often falls by the wayside. Parishioners are incredibly generous. Jean, our parish administrator, had got used to the particular clink of bags left in the office, and by Christmas Eve I had enough bottles of gin, wine and whisky to ensure that January would be anything other than dry. My flat looked like Princess Margaret's recycling bin.

As the gifts began to pile up, Christmassy panic set in: how was I going to (a) keep track of who had given what and (b) find time to buy presents in return? Given that my diary in December was covered with so many unintelligible entries that it less resembled a guide to my week and more a painting by Jackson Pollock, and that I was *just* about finding time to eat and breathe, neither seemed likely. As forty-five bunches of hastily purchased petrol-station flowers loomed as a seeming inevitability, one of our kindly churchwardens took me aside and revealed the mysteries of clerical gift-receiving. These gifts, I was told, were given in recognition that we wouldn't be having a 'proper' Christmas of our own. The congregation understood this and the booze was the least they could do by way of consolation.

So, it seemed, presents were a form of festive anaesthesia. As for the food side of things, Crispin warned me that it was only as they approached their teens that his two sons had learned what a traditional Christmas lunch was. Until then they had thought it was a bacon sandwich. With both parents ordained and busy, a mountain of turkey, stuffing, spuds and the rest was never going to be viable. Another cleric I know has taken up the custom of many Jewish families on Christmas Day and orders in an enormous Chinese takeaway. Who needs Brussels sprouts when you've got bean sprouts, eh?

As it happens, I did get my Christmas dinner that first year, and in subsequent ones as well. As a single clergyman, I wasn't even expecting a family Chinese or a gathering around a bacon sandwich. After the church was shut and people had made their way home, whistling the final carol, the only one who would be left was me.

I'd reconciled myself to the idea that, for the rest of my life, Christmas would consist of a nap, a microwave ready meal and a half-watched *Carry On* film. But it wasn't to be. Over the years families from various congregations have kindly invited me to join them. From the infectious joy of a Liverpool family Christmas to being fed champagne in Chelsea until I could barely stand, I have been treated to a chocolate-box selection of some of the best possible celebrations. Of them all, though, that first year will always stay with me. After we'd got through Midnight Mass, after we'd finished the morning service and finally sung 'Yea, Lord, we greet thee, born *this* happy morning' at something approaching an appropriate time and after I'd been welcomed, warmly, genuinely, as one of the family, by people I'd known for only six months or so, I staggered home through an empty city.

It was the middle of the night. Christmas Day had slipped away for another year and the feast of Stephen (Boxing Day to most of us) was still just a theoretical truth found on twenty-four-hour clocks. I was filled with wine and turkey. I contained more cheese than a French mouse's fridge. Although I felt fit to burst physically, it was a moment of release: my diary was as clear for the next few days as it could possibly have been and I knew that, courtesy of the charity of which Crispin was a patron, even our more transient members had had a good Christmas meal. I revelled in the fact that it would be forty-eight weeks before I had to sing 'O Little Town Of Bethlehem' again.

I went back to my flat and, as I collapsed on to my bed,

did something that had seemed unthinkable just twenty-four hours before: I reached for the Bible and read the Nativity story one last time. I'd thought I'd been inoculated against its narrative and, frankly, against its message, but I was wrong. I lay there and, as I read, I felt the distinct, and unexpected, beginnings of wetness in my eyes. These were not tears of anger at my own stupid sense of being bored of it or because of some crisis of faith but, I suppose, a response to its power. I wept in acknowledgement that, even though I'd heard it what felt like a million times before, it still worked. It told of the welcome of strangers, of unlikely people in unlikely places, of gifts, of waiting and longing and of the unexpected. Above all, of course, it was a story that told, that still tells, of the strange hallowing of the human condition. All in the form of a baby on a midwinter's night.

My Christmas might now have become a parade of the strange and the awkward, the chaotic and the far from home, the weirdly dressed and the totally unexpected, but on that particular December night, as I rehearsed that well-known story once again, it occurred to me that the first Christmas wasn't too dissimilar. That first Christmas had been characterized by the kindness and hospitality of strangers, and by encountering a touch of the Divine in the very human. As I drifted off to sleep I felt as if I *was* in the right place, and at the right time. Perhaps Christmas vicar-ing wasn't so bad. Perhaps chaotic Christmases are closer to the reality of God than we like to think. Perhaps I had had a proper Christmas after all.

8.

Ketamine and Assemblies

EPIPHANY

It was New Year's Eve and I was at a party. It was like lots of gatherings I attended in my twenties, taking place just a little further along a London Tube line than was convenient and consisting of too much drama to be relaxing but not enough to be interesting. I stumbled out of the glass doors of a friend's flat on to the square foot or so of patio that served as a garden. The chorus of Queen's 'Fat Bottomed Girls' still ringing in my ears,* I paused, cooled down and caught my breath as the party raged behind me. Suddenly I was aware that I wasn't the only one who'd sought respite from the hot breath and boozy sweat of the rave going on indoors. A man, probably my age or a little older, was outside with me.

---

* What is it about New Year's Eve parties that tempts even the artiest, most up-to-date music lovers to shelve their normal preferences and play unmitigated cheese?

In silence we stood, soaking up the last few moments of the year in the cool solitude of the patio garden.

After a while, as Freddie Mercury's final poetic tributes to oversized female posteriors faded into the next song, he turned to me. 'All right, mate – are you the guy with the coke?'

It took me a moment to realize he wasn't talking about the sugary liquid that first convinced everyone that Father Christmas wears red.* So it was that I marked my first secular New Year as a clerk in holy orders by being mistaken for a drug dealer. Clearly I gave off the air of a man heavily doped: after I'd let him down gently and told him I wasn't carrying a bag of Colombian marching powder inside the Book of Common Prayer, he then proceeded to ask whether I 'fancied a bit of ket'.

Now, a clergyman is routinely given things he doesn't want. I've been offered and accepted cups of tea so anaemic that I've been tempted to call the NHS 111 helpline. I've soldiered my way through bowls of soup that seemed to include hair as the primary ingredient. I even knew one colleague who valiantly accepted a Hobnob dampened by the piss of one of the feral cats that inhabited the house of the lady he was visiting. You also

---

* A liturgically incorrect marketing ploy: clergy have long worn white or gold vestments for the feast of Christmas and the twelve days after it (yes, that again . . .). St Nicholas would probably have worn something very itchy and, given that many ancient Mediterranean cultures washed their clothes using ammonia gathered from urine, probably with a slight yellow hue. Doubt that'd sell as much Coke, though.

learn the most effective way to say no. On some days, when I was visiting seven or eight parishioners, if I had accepted every single cup of tea or coffee offered, I'm sure I would have developed some sort of critical bladder condition. Refusing refreshment from a lady of a certain age is not an easy task, so I and many other vicars have long since devised a stock of appropriate phrases. These vary from the white lie, 'Thank you so much but I've just had one,' to the more earthily expressed truth – which was valued in Liverpool – of 'If I have that I'll piss myself on the way home.' I have to confess, though, that this particular suggestion at the party left me a bit stumped. I mean, it's hardly the same as turning down a slice of quiche at a fete, is it?

I decided to say no with the phrase I use when I'm accosted by people selling things on the street. Perhaps it's that collar again, but hawkers seem to gravitate to me as an easy target, and I'm afraid they all get exactly the same response.

'The end is near when the Lord will come again and visit this world with fire! Have you heard and repented?'

'It's all right, thanks. I'm C of E.'

'Comrade, would you consider joining the Labour Party's boycott of Israeli goods?'

'It's all right, thanks. I'm C of E.'

'Hello, sir, have you considered whether you might need a new life-insurance policy?'

'It's all right, thanks. I'm C of E.'

See? It's fail-safe.

I remember once, when I was still at theological

college, being on the bus between Oxford and Cambridge.* As we stopped at Bedford – which is, for reasons
best known to itself, a hub of Mormon activity – a gaggle
of Latter Day Saints got on.† Now, as my oft-used riposte
suggests, I'm sufficiently C of E to know that striking up
conversations with strangers on buses is more likely to
get you tasered in this country than to win converts to
the faith but I gather that a sort of can-do enthusiasm,
even in the face of such terrifying odds, is a key part of the
Mormon brand. So it was that these fresh-faced, white-
shirted ambassadors made their way up the coach, being
politely ignored by most of the passengers. I have to confess I wasn't in a particularly good mood: I'd just sat a
shedload of exams on subjects as diverse as the Creation
narrative in Genesis and the German theologian Karl
Barth's views on historical criticism. Put another way, the
last thing I wanted to talk about was *more* religion.

Perhaps, I thought, if I was doing something else
they'd be too polite to bother me. I scrabbled around in
my bag and pulled out the first two things my hands

---

* The official C of E stance on Purgatory can be found in
Article 22 of the 39 Articles of Religion, which states that
Purgatory, the intermediate state that Roman Catholics
believe most of us enter when we die, is a 'Romish doctrine'
and 'a fond thing vainly invented'. If anything has shaken
my faith in that Article it is a bus journey on the
X5 stopping service between Oxford and Cambridge.

† I don't know what the correct collective noun for members
of the Church of Latter Day Saints is: a purity of Mormons?
A prophecy of Mormons? A polygamy of Mormons?

could grab. Fate or Divine providence meant I alighted upon a copy of the New Testament in Greek (from which I had been revising for an exam) and a warm can of Stella Artois. I don't know whether it was the risk of having to debate with such a theologically engaged brain (ha-ha) or the fact that I was now consuming a warm lager at ten thirty in the morning but either way, on that occasion, the Mormons passed me by.

To return to that fateful patio some years later: despite my deployment of this trustiest of excuses, being mistaken for a drug dealer was about the most exciting thing to happen to me on that, or any other, New Year's Eve. As someone whose life is now bound by the rhythm of a year, a cycle of festivals, fasts and feasts, I feel like I should 'get' New Year. I don't. It's something of a nothing night, a moment we feel we have to imbue with organized fun for the sake of it. It's staying awake to drone along to the four words you actually know of 'Auld Lang Syne' with people you barely know. It's starting a whole new round of 365 days with a mouth like an ashtray and the lurking fear you said something embarrassing the night before. It's arguing about whether you put white wine or salt on a red wine stain in a carpet. It's warm champagne. It's the *Hootenanny*. It's the depressing corporate ice-breaking exercise of the calendar.

There is, however, some days later, a festival that *does* mean something, even if it's not as well known as Christmas and only celebrated in churches. While the rest of the world is settling into the misery of Dry January or preparing to break whatever resolution they've chosen to mark a new year with, the Church has a sort of Christmas Round Two: 6 January, twelve nights after the feast of the Nativity, is the feast known as Epiphany. It's still a word we occasionally use to describe a moment of revelation, be that realizing you're in love or remembering where you left your car keys. Contrary to the normal flow of a Nativity play, where all the events of the Christmas story happen within about fifteen minutes, Epiphany marks the visit of the Wise Men. It's known as the 'revelation of Christ to the Gentiles' as they were the first non-Jewish people to encounter Him. In the C of E it's viewed as the end of the Christmas season, hence the traditional removal of decorations, but in many churches, especially in the Orthodox tradition, it's a much bigger event, often marked as Christmas itself. In short, Epiphany has more cultural oomph than you might initially think as 6 January flies by in a flurry of kale smoothies, jogging and regret. Epiphanies are much better than resolutions anyway.

Epiphany is also the feast closest to when children return to school. It's one of those skeleton-in-the-closet moments when you realize that a lot more Christianity is lurking about the shape of life in the United Kingdom than we perhaps care to admit. There's no secular reason why kids shouldn't be in school on 1 January or, for that matter, 25 December, but the run of great feasts after Christmas – St Stephen, the Holy Innocents, St John the Evangelist and more – culminating in Epiphany makes as obvious a pivot point into a new term as any.

It was around this time of year, as Epiphany loomed and it became upsettingly clear that January wouldn't be going anywhere, that I conducted my first solo school assembly as a clergyman. Schools play much more of a part in ministry than you might expect. Just under 30 per cent of all primary schools are run by the Church of England and, for some parishes, school work is at the heart of how they serve their community. The intention of these endeavours (and often, it has to be said, the successful effect) is to give kids a solid start in life, grounded in the principles of loving their neighbour and serving their communities. My own school had not been a Church establishment but I had spent three months prior to being ordained as a classroom assistant in a short-staffed school in Manchester. That aside, it had been a very long time since I had been anywhere near a school of any sort – and the last occasion had been to celebrate leaving it.

I was a little nervous therefore when, in the shadow of Epiphany, I found myself in a school hall full of primary children. Especially as they sat in front of me maintaining an impassive, almost threatening, silence. Most were looking at their shoes or idly staring out of the large plate-glass windows. There was, however, one exception. A boy in the front row, probably no older than four or five, had locked me into a staring competition while he, slowly and expertly, picked his nose. I was meant to be engendering a calm and prayerful atmosphere at the beginning of the school day: a single candle had been lit, some gentle music was playing through a speaker, I had been presenting an air of studied holiness from my very first entrance to the school. Yet all of this was now derailed by the focal point of the assembly becoming an elaborate nose-picking masterclass.

Slowly but surely other children began to notice the nasal mining taking place in the front row. Other pupils, stirred from daydreaming, began to poke each other and pick or pretend to pick their noses in joyful imitation. I began to wonder whether I could use this to illustrate the talk I was supposed to be giving about the manifestation of Christ to the Gentiles. It was a metaphor for how God seeks us out, perhaps. Something about the depth of God's love? Things only calmed down when the head teacher strode in and immediately informed the original child, who had kept an uneasy eye contact with me throughout, that his chosen hobby was 'disgusting'. I went ahead with my original assembly about the arrival of the Wise Men but we all knew I'd been upstaged.

Never work with children or animals is an old show-business adage, but one that might also apply to the ministry. The problem is, while you might find a way of artfully cancelling a pet blessing service (not every cleric can be a latter-day St Francis), you're unlikely to escape ministering to school-aged children. Sunday Schools feature in almost all churches, and it's often the role of the junior priest to help coordinate activities and stories. Often the carefully crafted results of these sessions present an interesting theological challenge: while I don't think there's much harm in colouring Jesus's robe bright pink or a lurid green, there may be an issue with drawing a pair of horns on his head. Trying to introduce drama isn't much better. I know of one miniature St Stephen who decided he wasn't going to take his martyrdom by stoning lying down and began to pick up the gently lobbed pebbles around him and throw them back with considerable force. As one exasperated mother helping to supervise once told me, 'Most of it is just hoping they don't violently shit themselves.'

Obviously, there is a wide range of methods as to how one approaches the inevitable breaching of the old show-biz rule. Various clergy colleagues have modelled fascinating methods of dealing with children over the years. One nonchalantly interrupted a talk to a group of year-three kids to take delivery of a recently deceased parishioner's ashes. I'm not sure he ever explained what was in the 'special box' that arrived midway through 'He's Got The Whole World In His Hands'.

Before I was ordained, I was sent along to see an assembly conducted by a veteran of the genre, to see best practice modelled, to use the sort of corporate phrase Church communications now thrive on. I sat there as the elder priest began talking to the children about the love of God. So far, so safe. Things soon took a different turn.

'Of course, children, another thing St Paul tells us is that the love of God is SHARP. Do you know what else is sharp? This!'

The priest, who had previously been a missionary in Zululand, pulled out an enormous machete. A teacher gasped. The children sat totally unfazed.

'Now, to show you how sharp it is, I need a volunteer.'

Little hands shot up. Was I about to witness an appalling act of religio-psychotic violence?

Of course not. The children were given a series of soft fruits and encouraged to throw them towards the priest, who sliced them in half in mid-air, to squeals of delight from the assembled school. Was it a conventional assembly? No. Did it conform to any health and safety rulings? Also no. Will those children ever forget the sharpness of the love of God? A third no, I think.

The New Year/Epiphany period was an appropriate time to begin my school ministry. School is, at its best, all about giving kids a fresh or better start than they might have had without it. A Church school, specifically, is about contextualizing that in the teaching of Jesus to love our neighbours. Of course, like those New Year resolutions begun with the very best of intentions, that doesn't always work. The reality is that, while they'll probably still remember the tune of 'Shine Jesus Shine', they're probably also quite likely to respond in the age-old way when confronted with religion later on: 'No, thanks. I'm C of E.' Like it's a quiche or ketamine. I think part of me wanted to be different, to reverse that association and to make sure that my assemblies were producing good, enthusiastic Anglicans. I didn't exactly envisage myself as some sort of kindergarten Billy Graham but I was hoping I might see some of the immediate fruits of my labours.

As with so much of ministry, though, I learned that school work was about gently sowing seeds rather than blunt (or sharp) instrument indoctrination. If the kid who excavated his nose feels, however many years down the line, a pang of comfort at a relative's funeral, an urge to stroll into a church for a moment of calm, a quiet sense of the Divine in the midst of some moment of despair, then that Epiphany assembly won't have been a waste.

After all, the message of Epiphany is about an unlikely seed being sown among people who least expected it all those years ago.

Epiphany is about encounter as well, about reminding people that the Christian faith is not a hobby lived in isolation but about the messiness of living alongside each other. Meeting others is a good thing, of course, though sometimes difficult for a young priest. The round of New Year parties and the trend for entering the grimness of January with a round of hedonism weren't the only moments when vocation clashed with socializing. The long nights of January were often made more palatable by invites to parties. Being ordained in my twenties meant my first years of ministry coincided with a flurry of housewarmings, new-job drinks and engagement parties.

In fairness, way back during that first summer of wearing the collar, I'd enticed all my friends from across the country to Liverpool to celebrate my ordination with endless rounds of drinks and dubious encounters with hen parties: now it was payback time. It was always difficult. To other people weekends were a glorious forty-eight hours in which to indulge their interests or vices. For me they were the warm-up and then the Church equivalent of the 'big game'. Most Sunday mornings, while my mates shared their McDonald's breakfast orders over WhatsApp, I'd be sharing my often ill-formed thoughts on the Gospel according to St John.

That said, the realities of church work when I was feeling a little worse for wear on a Sunday morning were not unfamiliar to me in those first six months. I can tell you that a faceful of incense at ten o'clock in the morning is *not* a hangover cure and you should never allow anyone to tell you otherwise. I did begin to wonder whether it was possible to be young and take part in all (or, rather, almost all) the social occasions and engagements this entailed and still be a priest. The average age of a vicar in the year I was ordained was fifty-two and a half. I was just under half that total when the bishop had laid hands on me the previous summer. It had become clear, as that New Year dawned, that I would have to tone down some aspects of the partying. Or learn to say, 'No, thanks. I'm C of E', when a Jägerbomb was proffered. So I made an Epiphany resolution: to rebalance things.

In practice, this meant moderation rather than total abstention from invites, although I always turned down well-meant offers of narcotics. It became a bit of a ritual – turning up for the very start of a party on a Saturday night, then having to make my excuses to catch the last train home just as festivities were really getting under way.* On the occasions when an invite came through on a Friday, things would go fine until the inevitable question was asked, 'What do you do?' often followed by 'What are you doing here?' as if some memo about priests not having

---

* One wise priest did tell me that making an early exit is, in fact, an important clerical skill. If you're invited to the family bunfight – or actual fight, as the case may be – after a wedding or christening or funeral, not to stay for one drink looks churlish but to stay for six looks like you're a dangerous pisshead. Consequently the art of making oneself scarce after a couple of drinks is one of the subtle talents of ministers.

a social life had apparently been sent to every tipsy party attendee aged between twenty-four and thirty except, weirdly, me. Ineluctably, the question I started this book with — 'And what made you become a *priest*?' — would follow. These conversations would then, depending on the amount of alcohol consumed, descend into apologies for whatever view my conversation partner had of God.

Now, I'm not one to turn down an opportunity to share the faith, but I did question the mission value of such conversations. After all, I didn't corner them on their days off and spill my opinions on the financial markets or advertising or management consultancy. Consequently, extricating myself, as the conversation returned to religion, was often my primary objective on those winter evenings.

It wasn't long after I'd made my Epiphany resolution that I had, well, an epiphany.* I'd gone to London again for a friend's birthday celebrations. It was another of those bleak midwinter evenings and, once again, I'd stepped out on to a patio of a flat somewhere at the further reaches of a Tube line. I took a good lungful of air and began to calculate when I needed to make my escape. Suddenly the noise from the party intruded on the quiet of the night as a fellow guest slipped out of the glass doors and stood next to me, lighting a cigarette.

---

* There is a magnificently accurate Woody Allen quote about this: 'If you want to make God laugh, tell him your plans.' St Paul's letter to the Galatians puts it a little differently but comes to much the same conclusion: 'God is not mocked.'

Oh, good, I thought, a repeat of my *Miami Vice* moment at New Year. What will this one offer me? A bag of cocaine, perhaps? A vial of heroin? As long as it wasn't a quiche. We made small-talk for a while until the inevitable surfaced: 'And what do you do?' When I revealed my profession, I wasn't met with some sneering teenage atheism, or with a lewd joke, but with an unburdening of emotions. It isn't my place to say what, exactly, we talked through, but at the end of our chat, as I embraced my new acquaintance, even I, stone-hearted cynic that I am, had a distinct dampness in my eye.

Saying 'No, thanks. I'm C of E' isn't really an option when someone bares their soul to you. It doesn't really matter whether that happens in a church or on a patio of a flat somewhere towards the end of a Tube line. For all its faults, the Church is called to be where people are, and where they need it to be. The Church of England is the organization, the bishops, the cathedrals and the pomp, but it's also people, lay and ordained, meeting need where they see it, often in unlikely places. After all, Epiphany was about something bigger being found in an unlikely place. If I was the unlikely tipsy face of the C of E – of Christianity, even – to that person on the patio step, it was just as much a part of my ministry as preaching my sermon the next day. It didn't help with the hangover when the next day came but I think I was probably in the right place. As I said at the start, epiphanies are much better than resolutions anyway.

9.

Brute Beasts and Self-service

What's the most romantic thing you can think of? Flowers? Chocolates? Those weird bath bombs that children end up eating because they smell like sweets? Whatever the list of 'most romantic' consists of, I'm pretty certain that 'a severed head' isn't among them.* Yet having his head cut off is about the only real attribute the patron saint of love has. St Valentine is probably one of the best-known saints in the secular world. Almost every person in this country will know that his feast day is 14 February, even if they learned the hard way after having to sleep on the sofa one year. Ask people when St John the Baptist's Day is and they'll look at you as if you

---

* Or at the very least it features somewhere very low down on that list.

are a time traveller from 1468 trying to work out when and where you've landed.*

Perhaps that's unfair on Valentine. We know a bit more about him, namely the reason *why* his head was lopped off. He was supposedly a bishop or a priest in Rome during the early period of Christianity, an era when being part of the Church didn't mean getting up early on Sundays and volunteering for rotas but coming face to face with the sharp end of a lion. Valentine spent his ministry secretly helping his flock in any way he could but particularly by marrying couples in Christian ceremonies. The legend says he would cut out little hearts from paper and send them to those he had wed to remind them of their wedding vows. The Roman Empire, unfortunately, took a dimmer view of such activity than today's greeting-card manufacturers: Valentine was arrested and beheaded on 14 February. Love's never easy, is it?

February, a uniquely miserable month, is a weird time to celebrate love. It's before spring's explosion of natural reproduction, long outside the sultry romance of summer, too far gone from the beauty of autumn's changing colours or even from the need to keep one another warm in December or January. In fact, if you had to choose the least sexy, least romantic, least love-filled month on the facts of weather and atmosphere alone, you'd surely choose February. It's up there – or, rather, down there – with severed heads. Then again, there's no

---

* St John the Baptist's Day is, of course, 24 June. Now, tell me, what's the latest score in the Wars of the Roses?

accounting for the taste (or, more accurately, the sched-
uling) of Roman imperial executioners. So it was that we
came to mark romance and relationships at this particular
time of year. The fact that there is now some doubt in the
Church around Valentine's historical existence hasn't
been passed on to the rest of the world. The Roman
Catholic Church has removed any observation of him at
this time of year, with only the tiniest regional excep-
tions for Malta and a town in Italy, so dubious are they of
his existence. The Church of England still honours him,
especially in its traditional calendar of saints. The more
modern update mentions him too, although it registers
the option of remembering St Cyril and St Methodius,
bearded twins who invented Slavic languages, instead.
Still, despite all this, the Valentine cult lives on in a big
way. It is, I think, one of the few cases of the secular
world being keener to hang on to ancient religious tradition than the Church.

A lot of my time as a young cleric was spent dealing with
Valentine's-type love.* Unfortunately, as what you've just
read might *faintly* have suggested, I am not one of life's natural romantics. Yet since those early Christian days the
Church has been involved in weddings, the apex points of
romantic love. Valentine might have been a martyr for

---

* Every 15 February (or the Sunday morning closest to that
  date) we had to deal with a less romantic form of Valentine's-
  type love as our church garden gathered up the leftovers of a
  Valentine's night out in the city centre: discarded love-heart-
  shaped accessories, deflated penis-shaped balloons and, of
  course, the occasional used condom.

marriage, but in terms of romance overload – and even physical violence – the gorily dispatched saint's feast day was nothing compared to some of the weddings. In the weeks around Valentine's Day we did our wedding preparation for all the couples we would be marrying in church that year. It was always a diverse collection of the betrothed – young and old, first and second marriages, the devoutly Christian and the generally indifferent, nervous grooms and the occasional bridezilla. We gathered them all in church where a series of ice-breakers helped them begin – or so my colleagues and I hoped – to think about what might be different about getting married in a church rather than a hotel or golf club or register office.

Wedding preparation had its awkward moments: sitting down with a couple and going through the purposes of marriage for one. If working out what marriage is for is a weighty enough theological question, it's an even weightier practical one. Once you've got all the lovey-dovey parts out of the way the subject of sex rears its head. Not something anyone really wants to be discussing with a vicar of any age. In fairness, most clergy feel just as awkward: nothing makes you feel more like a third wheel than having to talk about what modern liturgy calls 'the tender joy of sexual union'. It didn't take me long to paraphrase that bit in the weddings I did. As is often the case, the old liturgy puts it better: the preface in the Book of Common Prayer defines our sexual appetites as being 'like brute beasts with no understanding'.

The preparation we provided had many more aspects than this – the questions of flowers or music often ended up being much more important – but they rarely made people blush in quite the same way. What was at the heart of the preparation was helping the couples to discern what married life – and specifically married life begun in the context of a wedding in church – was going to look like, warts and all.

Alongside the weddings I had to prepare for and conduct in a professional capacity, I was asked to take a lot of friends' weddings. One of the joys and challenges of being ordained just as your friends are all jumping headlong into the world of matrimony is that they immediately wonder, 'Who of our recently ordained acquaintances can conduct our wedding according to the rites of the Church of England?' This required its own brand of wedding prep: I had to sit, like some wingman, while the couple looked adoringly at each other and got excited about the big day. My job was mostly to steer things back in the direction of cold, hard sanity when star-crossed lovers found themselves dancing with disaster.

I had many stock responses in my arsenal:

'Yes, the T-shirts were hilarious on the stag do, but I don't really think they're *quite* right for the ushers in church, do you?'*

---

* I attended several of the stag dos of friends I married, which, while not quite a conflict of interest, put me in the occasional sticky spot. I awoke on the second morning of one such stag do on a canal boat somewhere in Oxfordshire. The next few hours were spent desperately, and unsuccessfully, trying to stop said canal boat from taking on water after it had careered into a lock that morning.

'I'm sure he *is* a very good dog but do you really want to trust him with the rings?'

'Please, please, don't spend *too* long in the pub before-hand. You have to be sober for me to marry you.'

Wedding planners charge God only knows how much to tell people to buy a slightly more expensive type of table setting, while clergy find themselves advising on every aspect of the wedding, from questions of dubious legality (although I am still yet to have anyone attempt bigamy on me) to where to sit awkward relatives at the reception. I'm not sure this is part of the official role but I suppose it must be nice to talk to someone who has been through multiple weddings in a different way from, say, Elizabeth Taylor or Henry VIII. On the whole, though, it was less playing the kill-joy and more guiding people through the perils and pitfalls of the service.

Readings and hymns were occasionally areas of pre-marital tension. Fortunately, I spent the lead-up to Valentine's and the kick-off of wedding preparation devising a handy guide.

A DEFINITIVE RANKING/ASSESSMENT OF
WEDDING HYMNS

Hymn : 'All Things Bright And Beautiful'
Popular with : people who haven't been to church
   since school, people who enjoy sniggering at
   'purple-headed mountain', Victorian child
   ghosts.

Wedding suitability : see above re. 'purple-headed mountain'.*

Volume at which usually sung : ranges from mumbled semi-silence for the verses to 'lost child screaming in the middle of a shopping centre' for the chorus.

Hymn : 'Amazing Grace'
Popular with : early-nineteenth-century abolitionists, soul singers, brides called 'Grace'.
Wedding suitability : given it was written by a former slave trader who saw the evil of his ways, it isn't *especially* marital in its themes.
Volume at which usually sung : either low respectful groan or great swelling crescendo, nowhere in between.

Hymn : 'Guide Me O Thou Great Redeemer'
Popular with : the Welsh, people who gain pleasure from doing the repetition of the 'feed me now and ever more' bit, uncles who've had too much in the pub beforehand.
Wedding suitability : the final verse is all about dying but, hey, it gets people singing.

---

* I once conducted a christening at which an Oscar-winning actor was in the congregation. I am very pleased to report that they, too, sniggered at Mrs C. F. Alexander's clunky penile imagery.

Volume at which usually sung: mostly 'very loud', ranging up towards 'close proximity to Cape Canaveral rocket launch'.

Hymn: 'Love Divine, All Loves Excelling'
Popular with: people who watched the Royal Wedding in 2011 and decided to copy their hymns, Methodists.
Wedding suitability: it mentions love a lot, but it specifically points out that God's love is better than any human love – including romantic love – in the first line.
Volume at which usually sung: midpoint between bellow and yell.

Hymn: 'Jerusalem'
Popular with: rugby fans, Last Night of the Proms-goers, those who are obsessed with changing the National Anthem.
Wedding suitability: zero, unless you're a descendant of William Blake or on the England front row.
Volume at which usually sung: Twickenham at three-quarters capacity, when everyone is four beers down.

Readings could be just as fraught as hymns with potential difficulties. I will never forget the look of stoic resignation on the face of one rugby player I married as the entire congregation watched him drop a single tear during a reading from *Winnie-the-Pooh*. Tear-jerking children's books aside, all church weddings require at least one reading from the Bible, so giving advice on that became a key part of the wedding gig. Most people who get married in church are not regular churchgoers, yet they understand that what they're entering into is a serious, sacred business so many still come to the Church for the main event. While this is a great privilege, it means that several have no real idea about the Bible, let alone which bits are more or less appropriate for a wedding ceremony. Unlike with the hymns, it seemed possibly sacrilegious to rank bits of actual Holy Scripture. Also, there wasn't any point: the number one most popular reading by a country mile was, of course, from 1 Corinthians: 'Love is patient, love is kind.' People tended to eschew readings from the fruitier bits of the Bible – although I did have a couple who selected a very raunchy reading from the Song of Songs, which talks about how a male figure referred to as 'my beloved' thrusts his hand into a perfumed opening. Unsurprisingly it's not a passage that they cover very often in Sunday School. Better to stick with 'Love is patient, love is kind.' Not even St Paul at his most optimistic said it would be easy, though.

In Corinthians, St Paul is actually talking about a different love from the Valentine's Day chocolate, flowers, teddy-bear love. It's closer to the love of St Valentine – one of sacrifice and suffering. In this regard weddings are tough. At the heart of having to preach on that exact passage was the challenge of having to model and preach a concept of love that is deeper and more sacrificial than conventional romantic love, while also not glowering over a joyful occasion. It isn't that romantic love is bad, or even that it's not Christian, it's just that the love of the Bible isn't a fuzzy feeling: it's something almost terrifyingly powerful. Put another way, I wouldn't have gone through the previous ten months or so for the sake of the commercialized vision we're sold as love or even, frankly, sex. A much deeper Divine love is what keeps me in the midst of the madness that is ministry.

But there is the quandary I'm stuck with as I look out over wedding congregations: how do you remind people that it's about more than flowers or intercourse while not coming across as some sex-obsessed puritanical maniac? The traditional vows help here: to have and to hold, in sickness and in health, till death us do part. They are deep, redolent phrases and promises the couple are asked to make. They don't speak of fluffiness but of sacrifice. Most of the time I find it best to let these ancient words speak for themselves. Oh, and at no point do they mention 'the tender joy of sexual union'. Thank God.

Assuming the prep passes without all parties involved dying of embarrassment, there's the wedding service itself. As the writing career of Richard Curtis demonstrates, gathering a (hopefully) besotted pair of lovers, two extended families and a group of friends with varying blood-alcohol levels is an endless source of potential pitfalls. The weddings I found myself taking in that first year featured the full panoply of characters: late brides, a pair of guests who managed to turn up on the wrong day, even a marriage that was nearly derailed by an elderly relative who unleashed a bout of very loud flatulence every time the congregation were required to sit down or stand up, resulting in a fit of giggles that spread across the assembled friends and family like wildfire. By the time I was on the final 'Please stand' several people had had to leave or face the ire of the bride and/or an aneurysm.

As February began and Valentine's name loomed large once again in the calendar, I wondered whether the martyred saint himself had ever had to deal with Roman equivalents of wedding mishaps. I can't imagine brides who had to tell the time by sundials were any less given to late arrivals. I can't imagine that relatives who existed on a diet of stuffed dormice and ostrich tongues were any less flatulent either.

Being around all this love, even if it isn't the sort of love that is at the heart of a priest's calling, has its effect, even on a cleric. Since the Reformation, when Archbishop Cranmer supposedly shipped his German wife secretly to England in a big crate, the Church of England has allowed clergy to marry.* Indeed, it's now considered a bit odd for clergy not to have a partner. While there's a stock character of a vicar in people's minds, there's arguably even more of a stock character as a vicar's spouse. Jam,

---

* Of course, clerical celibacy, the practice of forbidding clergy to marry, was not introduced to Western Christianity until the mid-medieval period. Beforehand, for the seven hundred or so years of Christianity in this country, clergy with families was the norm. There have been priests with spouses in the English Church for longer than there haven't been.

'Jerusalem' and generally accommodating everyone who turns up on your doorstep. I know most clergy wives and husbands find such a caricature infuriating – after all, what's supposed to happen to the stereotype if a vicar falls in love with someone who likes smoking, drinking and dropping the word 'piss' into general conversation?* That's also the case for a number of clergy I know, so perhaps it's a case of swings and roundabouts.

I was ordained while single, and remained so for that whole first year. Again, I think February is a particularly cruel month to celebrate love, not only for those who must pretend that their tired, cold-sore-addled partner is at their most lovable. To be single and have to walk alone in the icy cold past all these celebrations of love, as saccharine as they may be, isn't a barrel of laughs. That's even more the case if it's your job to celebrate love, to prepare people for their weddings, and especially if it's considered suspicious if you don't have a partner. It'd be impossible for someone to live an entirely emotionally fulfilling existence off the snatched eroticism of being asked, as I once was, to 'heavily lubricate the hand-held microphone with hand sanitizer in between uses'. Also, February is bloody cold and sharing a bed saves on the central heating.

Whether it was frugality with regard to my boiler or, more likely I think, a morbid fear of being single in my

---

* I can think of numerous occasions where I would make a beeline for exactly these types as they were often much more fun than some of the clergy.

approaching thirties, it was around this time that I
thought I ought to try to get out there. Dating as a cleric
is weird. I mean, I was crap enough at it before I was
ordained, a poorly put-together mass of nerves, badly
timed jokes and too much aftershave. Add clerical angst
and you have a seriously unattractive package. That
looming, inevitable question 'What do you do?' is no
longer a chance to crack a joke at parties but the cue for a
look of total bemusement and/or horror as a lifetime of
village fetes, Victoria sponges and vicarage-based murder
investigations flashes before the eyes of someone who,
until then, you were getting on with quite well. Just my
luck to be the only person in their twenties to have their
love life ruined by Agatha Christie.*

So it was that I found myself walking back through
the February cold, past shops full of Valentine's tat, after
another date I was sure would lead nowhere. When
Christ attended the wedding at Cana in Galilee, I mused,
and turned the water into wine – his first miracle – could
anyone else have imagined He was setting in motion a
series of events that would lead to my lonely walk home
from a cocktail bar?† I wondered, too, what Valentine

---

* Unless there's an under-thirty organizer of Nile cruises or a
  similarly aged attendant on the Orient Express who's had
  similar trouble and is reading this. If so, solidarity.

† I have written 'anyone else' not to claim some foresight for
  myself but rather to acknowledge that part of what
  Christians believe about the nature of Christ is his
  foreknowledge, that he knew – knows – the beginning and
  the end of all. And I think it's fair to say that bigger sacrifices

had had in mind all those years ago when he first found himself gaining a name as the original matchmaker. I doubt it did his dating prospects any good either. I spent a lot of time talking about Divine love, that love of 1 Corinthians 13 and all those hymns, but I couldn't seem to navigate the love that everybody else was spending their whole time talking about. Perhaps, I concluded, romance did need a patron saint.

Valentine, interestingly, isn't only the patron of love. He has other areas of interest: epilepsy, beekeeping, and Lesbos, which was, of course, the home of the Ancient Greek writer Sappho. Her particular brand of erotic poetry led to the island's association with love between women, whence 'lesbianism'. How typical that a Church which ties itself in knots over what it terms 'same-sex attraction' could have appointed the same saint to be patron of the love it will bless and the home of a love it won't. I'm less convinced it's accidental. God has a funny way of correcting some of the Church's knot-tying by gentle hints that the unbelieving might see as mere coincidence.

That said, alongside the paradox there's real pain too. I knew of several clergy, including one without whose ministry I would probably never have been ordained,* who resigned their permissions to officiate at services in

---

have been made for the Gospel, not least by people like Valentine, than a few awkward dates.

* She and I regularly debate whether she did me a favour there or not.

parish churches (they can still officiate in places where the authority of the bishops has ancient limitations, such as Oxbridge colleges) so that they could enter into marriages with partners of the same sex. During that month of wedding preparation, my boss Crispin came into the office uncharacteristically angry. Not at me, although I had lost a strategic battle with the photocopier earlier that morning, but at the Church of England. He had just had to tell a couple, devout and devoted, that due to the Church's current fudge on same-sex weddings and despite his own feelings, they couldn't have their wedding in church as it was against the law.

Still, it remains that I can bless a parakeet or a burger van or a bin or nuclear weaponry (all actual examples) but could be faced with criminal charges and defrocked for doing the same for a couple, very much in love, who happen to have the same configurations below the belt. Also, put frankly, compared to the wider population, a disproportionate number of those who serve as clergy in the Church of England are gay. If it decided to boot out every gay priest because of whom they loved, 'We'd have to go self-service,' as the Queen Mother once said, when told to stop employing homosexuals at Clarence House. Practicality has won out over previous theology before – although I hope no colleagues of mine have any plans to bring a partner from Germany in a shipping crate.

That year, as Valentine's Day passed, yet another fight in the global Church loomed about sex. The Church seems doomed to talk about it until the very end of time. Judgement Day will be happening around us and we'll still be debating how we might 'go self-service'. So to speak. It's not, of course, that sex isn't important: the hijacking of St Valentine's Day into a celebration of it shows how important it is because the Church has something positive to say about it. The ancient concept that affection might be about more than the purely physical could probably do with another vigorous airing. It's worth noting, too, that Valentine isn't the patron saint of sex: he is the patron saint of couples who are in love.

Yet there were others – again without whom I would not have been ordained – for whom the Church to change its stance would be a departure from what they earnestly believe to be true. I love and respect them too. So what happens when people you love don't agree? You never see that mentioned in the Valentine cards, do you? Are there things that love truly cannot conquer? At root, that's something we've learned to accept with regard to romantic love – 'Irreconcilable differences', 'It wasn't meant to be' . . . But love Divine says there is nothing that the love of God can't breach. After all, what's a disagreement when this is the love that conquers death? That doesn't make any of it easy but then, as I said, love never is.

As those wedding preparation sessions ended and as the flowers, chocolates and teddy bears were consigned first to the reduced section in the supermarket, then to the skip, I found myself, to my surprise, less cynical about love than I had been before. Don't get me wrong: I'd still rather take a funeral than a wedding any day of the week, but I suppose I no longer viewed love as something to be

dismissed or vaguely embarrassed by. Indeed, I resolved
to make the message of love at the heart of all my preaching. It's one of those concepts that Jesus Christ talked
about a fair bit. Not so much the romantic love that I had
to hope would come to me in due time, despite my having taken the cloth and my own gaping personality flaws.
Rather, it was the love I felt had called me to continue
through the awkwardness, that had called all the priests I
knew and respected to continue through pastoral ill-
treatment and that had called Valentine to risk his life to
show a bit of it to couples all those years ago. Love that
I'd call Divine, and which all of us who'd entered its service had to believe was all other loves excelling. It struck
me that if that love could make a severed head a symbol
of romance, surely it could make a romantic of sorts out
of me.

IO.

Scratch Cards in the Wilderness

The first time I tried to give up alcohol for Lent I lasted exactly seven hours. I was a student, still having my first brushes with piety, and thought, when it came to acts of self-denial, it was best to throw myself in at the deep end. Go hard or go home. It was a catastrophe, of course. By mid-afternoon on Ash Wednesday I had a cold pint in my hand, preparing for another student night out of moronic chants, illegible club-entry stamps and lingering shame. Lent is supposed to be a time when the little things we love, our little vices, are put aside as a sign of our commitment to our faith. I was full of initial zeal for the new way of life I was committing to but couldn't resist the very first invite to the pub that had come my way. It didn't bode well.

Fast forward a few years: I was now ordained and facing a similar dilemma. Since that last attempt at Lenten rigour, I had undergone the privilege of ordination, my collar was

more comfortable round my neck, I had navigated funerals, weddings, Christmas. I had learned not to say 'piss' or
'bugger' in front of old ladies.* Unfortunately my willpower, or lack thereof, remained exactly the same. I knew,
deep down, that trying to give up booze was probably
futile. It wasn't that I was an alcoholic, scurrying back to
the vestry to drink turps between services, but rather that
visits to the pub, unguarded conversations over a pint, the
release of attending the odd party (and some of them were
very odd) was an important part of what I felt I was in the
parish to do. I was in a context where hospitality – be that
buying a round or giving someone a bottle of wine – was
taken seriously. To be seen to reject all that for the sake of
personal piety would not, I think, have done me much
good in the eyes of the people to whom I was ministering.
Especially when I inevitably failed midway. Fundamen-
tally, I didn't think going dry would do my ministry, or
my own spiritual life, any favours.

However, Lent was fast approaching. The question of
what I was intending to give up was already being asked
by members of the congregation and answering, 'Well,
not gin,' wouldn't wash. In the end, I settled to give up
two other great loves: meat and tobacco. I am not one of
life's natural vegetarians so choosing a salad or the beige

---

* I invariably found that a number of the older ladies in
congregations to whom I ministered used much fruitier
language than I ever dared deploy. I recall in one parish
hearing a rather distinguished lady bark, firmly but lovingly,
at her dawdling husband, 'Oh, do hurry up, dear, and stop
being such a daft old c**t.'

wobbliness of tofu over a steak would be a stretch for me personally but still attainable and so, I hoped, vaguely spiritually improving.

I was successful in this endeavour despite manifold temptations. After Lent began on Ash Wednesday, the McDonald's corporation seemed to go into an advertising overdrive. Every single bus stop and billboard I wandered past seemed to have a great glistening picture of a burger or some chicken nuggets, tempting me to break my discipline in return for a sinful meat treat. I prevailed. Just. Now, I know it's not quite the same as Satan taking Christ to the top of the mountain and offering him all the kingdoms of the world, but it was not without its impressiveness as a feat of willpower. Similarly, while I was not a regular smoker, the occasional puff of a cigarette at a party or, my favourite treat, a long drag of a cigar had become something I looked forward to. Consequently I resolved to abstain until Easter and, because Lent is also meant to be a time of alms-giving as well as abstinence, hand over the money I saved to a worthy cause. This, too, proved to be a success, and I gave great thanks to God when, on Easter evening, I smoked two cigarettes and a cigar at the same time, my mouth a horrible little temple to tobacco. Sometimes incense just doesn't take the edge off.

Over the years I have tried giving up many things. Booze, meat and tobacco were the big ones but I attempted other disciplines too, with varying degrees of success, from swearing to Twitter. The idea is that you might enjoy and appreciate the thing you have given up even more when you take it up again after Easter. One Greek Orthodox bishop, who, as that tradition dictates, took Lent exceptionally seriously and abstained from almost everything but bread and water, told me he found there really was no greater joy than a plump olive and a crumb of feta eaten on Easter morning. By contrast, former Archbishop of Canterbury Robert Runcie, when principal of a theological training college, asked his group of would-be vicars what they were going to do for Lent. Most offered pious answers – praying more, only reading the Bible, giving up alcohol, tobacco or television. One, either brave or foolish enough to answer candidly, told Runcie that his plan was to try to give up masturbation. There was a sharp, collective intake of breath as the ordinands awaited his reaction. Runcie, without batting an eyelid, simply tilted his head to one side, looked up to Heaven and said, rather ponderously, 'Well, what a wonderful way to spend Easter morning.'

Abstinence can undoubtedly be its own reward. Sometimes, though, the desire to abstain, then to compensate at Easter, goes too far. Louis, our parish assistant, was addicted to sweets and resolved to avoid them for the Lenten period. By way of recompense and to incentivize himself during the long, sugarless days and nights, he bought a giant gummy cola bottle, which sat in his office as a reward for the righteous rigour of his fast. Eventually Easter came and the enormous cola bottle, which was about the length and width of a toddler, was the centrepiece of the Easter celebrations. The only problem was how to eat it. In the end thin slices were carved off it, like a festive ham, and proffered to a frankly revolted congregation. Louis and I spent the following forty days of Easter (for there are, of course, forty days of feast after forty days of fast) trying to find new ways of eating this vast globule of gelatine without being sick. Eventually we marked Pentecost by throwing its gnawed and increasingly desiccated carcass into a nearby bin. All aspects of religious practice, however benign they might initially seem, can be taken too far, and the excess of E-numbers had proved no Easter treat at all.

Easter was also the time I found myself most inclined towards other little vices. Having given up things I truly loved, in the form of smokes and steak, I felt I could indulge a little more in more minor bad habits for which I had merely a passing affection. In that first Lent I took up playing scratch cards, courtesy of the National Lottery. It wasn't, I think, so much the thought that I might win some vast amount of cash and give up vicar-ing for ever. It was more the need for a small, manageable vice during the season of virtue. My grandmother had long used them as a way of keeping her grandchildren quiet – there is something mesmerizing about the removal of that thin layer of grubby foil. There is also a naughty thrill in such low-key gambling.

The only problem arose when I got a winner. It's still considered relatively bad form to go in and collect gambling winnings while wearing a dog collar.* On those

---

* A journalist once told me, while I was wearing a particularly thick, full, linen dog collar, that had I worn such at the races

occasions, I found myself giving those little tokens for one, two or five pounds to those who spent their days begging on the city's streets. One man, let's call him Chris, would struggle round the precincts of the hospital where I did most of my pastoral visiting. He was the main recipient of my winnings. In the end, I decided that I should forgo scratch cards in the season of abstinence, much to the disappointment of some of my friends on the streets. I found other ways to help them, but marking Lent, I decided, by taking up gambling, however low stakes it was, probably wasn't in the spirit of the season. Whether the giving up of this lesser vice did my moral compass any favours I couldn't say, but it certainly helped my bank balance.

Of course, Christians don't give things up in Lent for the sake of it or even, really, for the health or financial benefits. While the wider world still knows about Lent as a convenient time to indulge in a health kick or finally address a particular bad habit, the Church views it as something more. Lent lasts for forty days and forty nights, thus mirroring the time Jesus spent in the wilderness being tempted by the devil at the very start of his ministry. The idea is that, in preparation for Easter – the greatest of feast days – we enter into a wilderness ourselves, where we deny ourselves certain things and try to resist temptation as Christ did.

---

some time between 1910 and 1960 I would have been arrested on sight. Apparently it was a favourite disguise for undercover illegal bookies.

This is why we're encouraged to work out what our own wilderness might be, why we are encouraged to distance ourselves from some forms of pleasure and to give up certain little joys. Being 'in the wilderness' doesn't just mean being lost: it means taking time away from what is easy or comfortable. The truth is that wildernesses take lots of different forms. They aren't just about the desolation of not being able to have cake or booze or cigarettes for a chunk of the year. Indeed, there are times when the Church itself can feel pretty wilderness-like. A life in ministry can sometimes seem less like a jolly pilgrimage towards a joyful goal and more like a stagger through an inhospitable cultural landscape, with only the occasional mirage of hope and the constant threat of treading on a snake or some other dispenser of toxicity. Put another way, ministry in the twenty-first century can often seem like banging your head against a brick wall. I will never forget the look of the wilderness in the face of a clergyman when he was told during a meeting with other local clergy that the basement of his church had filled with raw sewage. Being up to your knees in effluent, trying to pump it out to save a listed building is about as far from the comfortable and the familiar as it is possible to be. These wildernesses of the soul are as much a part of Christian tradition as physical ones. It can be a little depressing to work for an institution that only ever makes any sort of headline when it's done something wrong or when its members are at each other's throats. I was only a lowly curate, the bottom rung of the ladder that had numerous vicars, deans, canons and bishops clinging to it, but even I encountered some of the less savoury conflicts that mark the life of the Church as a national institution.

It was at the very start of one Lent when I saw the institutional Church close up. Ash Wednesday is a day when penitence, the admission of our sins, both shared and individual, is front and centre in the Christian calendar. The 'Ash' in the title comes from the ancient practice, now widely revived, of drawing a cross in ash on the foreheads of those who seek penitence. The crosses can take various forms, depending on the finger-painting talent of the priest involved, from carefully planned and geometric to a random smear. As the ash is administered the priest says, 'Remember thou art dust and to dust thou shalt return.' It's a hugely powerful reminder of human mortality and, in its own way, rather comforting. It's especially good as an antidote to clerical pomp and circumstance as, crucially, the clergy are ashed as well.

On Ash Wednesday of this first Lent, we were due a visit from a clerical VIP. This figure arrived with a gaggle of assorted staff members crammed into a Volkswagen Sharan. Not quite the grand retinue of medieval cardinals, but there were five of them, which outranked our home team of rector and assistants. Our VIV (Very Important Vicar)* swept into our church and was talked through what he had to do during the service. Every time he wanted to query something he would dramatically wave

---

* This is actually how *Debrett's* advises you to address the dignified clergy.

SCRATCH CARDS IN THE WILDERNESS

an empty sparkling-water bottle – his constant companion – in the vague direction of the issue and expect a solution. It was my first encounter with a Prince of the Church and here he was, using a piece of litter as a wand, like a deranged bin wizard. If the priesthood has taught me anything it's that things – and people – are often not as you expect them. Sometimes that's a good and happy reminder of the breadth of humanity, but it can be disappointing too. When we took to the streets to inflict ash on people going about their day-to-day business, someone came up to me to ask whether this exalted figure, to whom we were in thrall, was Chris Eubank. I had to disappoint him.

I'm sure he wasn't the only person I've disappointed in my ministry. In fact there have been times when I have disappointed myself, and have felt disappointed in the idea of ministry. It rather comes with the territory if you're seeking to follow a figure who goes into the wilderness. But if an element of disappointment is simply part and parcel of the wilderness of Church life, then conflict is even more so. Collecting any group of people together with a supposedly common cause will invariably lead to disagreement. The sort of arguments that occurred at parish level, though – who had the keys to the loos in the parish centre, where we stored the kneelers, the speed at which the organist played 'Happy Birthday' – were often gentle reminders of human fallibility.

That isn't to say there weren't slightly higher-stakes reminders of human fallibility. I confess that prior to ordination, crime was something I hadn't encountered much before I put on a dog collar but afterwards it was round every corner. It wasn't just the Church that was filled with the disappointing and the sinful, it was humanity as a whole. However, for all the moping about the human condition that Lent encourages, it was difficult not to raise a smile at some of these incidents – it was as if even the criminal was destined to be paired with the comical.

A city-centre church is always going to attract the full spectrum of humanity and we were, on a semi-regular basis, subject to break-ins. My laptop was pilfered twice, once when I was midway through the unsaved draft of another book. I confess that my thoughts towards the culprit were not especially Christian. Neither was my language. I made up for my fury by joining the Home Guard-style attempts to burglar-proof the clergy offices. These included the random and ineffective application of masking tape to door frames and windows, wedging a harpsichord in the middle of a connecting corridor, installing bollards on the forecourt (which scythed through dozens of no-claims bonuses in a matter of weeks) and, famously, hiding in the office with all the lights switched off to see if we could catch our criminal on CCTV during a return attempt.

We weren't always on the active receiving end of crime. Our proximity to the law courts meant that each day numerous defendants, witnesses, wronged plaintiffs and lawyers passed through our doors. I recall one encounter when an animated man came up to me and asked, as so many did, for a prayer: 'It's for a defendant, Father, at the court today.'

'Of course. What's his n—'

'Except he didn't do it. Absolutely not. All a fix.'

'I'm sorry to hear that. Of course I'll pray for him. What's his name?'

'Max.'

'Is he a friend or relative?'

'No. He's me dog.'

Mindful of how much I'd cared for my dog as a child, I prayed for Max, and for his owner. I still never found out what he'd done but one of the key ideas of the wilderness is we're all in it together, be we clergymen or criminal canines. In short, the Church might be in a mess, but the rest of the world is too. These run-ins with the worldly wilderness were regular and healthy, a little reminder that the wilderness of the Church wasn't anything particularly special, and a prompt not to stick my head too deep into the purely spiritual desert sand.

In contrast to these day-to-day examples of human nature's imperfection – which we're meant to dwell on in Lent – the ones that cropped up in newspapers or in the General Synod seemed to be examples of pure venom. Social and mainstream media were full of fights that started in the Church or, more accurately, that the Church had started with itself. Whether it was about episcopal appointments or styles of worship or, the perennial favourites, money and sex, conflict seemed constant. It felt like a blow against the idea that the great enterprise I'd become involved in was worthwhile. Each fight, each scandal felt like another step into the wilderness.

In due time I would experience the dark side of the Church personally. After I left Liverpool I took up a new job down south. I'd been warned by friends and fellow clergy not to go to that particular church; the general culture was, in one priest's words, 'utterly toxic'. But I knew better, of course. If I'm honest, things started out okay. Nothing worked, time was endlessly wasted, vanity and pomposity were the norm, but those are all wildernesses I could live with. Soon, though, the creeping, more invidious wilderness of the soul began to sneak in: controlling, manipulative behaviour. I'd be humiliated at meetings, ignored in public, endlessly gossiped about. There was an atmosphere of desert, even of, dare I say it, wickedness.

I found that those I worked with in this particular church, at first honest with me about the toxic atmosphere, soon became hostile and cagey, with people at every level utterly caught up in the climate of fear and loathing. One thing was said behind backs, another in public. Explosions of anger and spat venom were the norm. Soon it became clear that I wasn't the only one who had suffered. I started getting phone calls, emails, messages on social media, the accounts eerily similar. It had gone on for years. I was shocked to be refused communion that Christmas, and it remains one of the most painful incidents of my life. Priests are meant to work in the wilderness, but when there's no way out, no redemptive arc, just more and more damaging behaviour, it becomes too much. And it becomes necessary to walk away.

This, in the end, is what I did, into another, different wilderness. But that's another story. Throughout that hideous year, I kept the memory of the happier years in Liverpool in my mind; a reminder that it didn't have to be like this, that wildernesses of the soul should be the toxic exception rather than the general rule.

Even the 'good guys' could and did disappoint, though. In Liverpool, I came face to face with one such just as we reached the denouement of Lent. One of the other traditions of the season, alongside public penitence, abstinence and alms-giving, is study. It was our habit during Lent to host speakers at church from a range of backgrounds, theological and otherwise, to stimulate study and respectful debate. I recall one visit by a campaigner for progressive causes – human rights, greater openness and accountability – in- and outside the Church. He gave an impassioned chastisement of the Church for its failure to support gay people properly within our communities. 'Oppression,' he said, 'is still happening because we say it is still happening.' It was clear that he, rightly, challenged the Church's assertion that it was listening when the very people it claimed to be listening to thought otherwise.

Over drinks after his fiery lecture, I asked him whether he thought this dynamic applied universally. Of course he did. He then proceeded to dismiss a different minority group who, at that time, were raising concerns about their treatment in the public sphere but who didn't fit his definitions. Universality has its limits, apparently. I left feeling more despondent.

As Lent progressed, I often glimpsed true despair,

when the atmosphere of decline and introspection, of seemingly intentional isolation of the Church from the needs of the people we were meant to serve became too much. A long slow glide into irrelevance seemed inevitable and would take superhumans to reverse it. Superhuman I was not.

I met up with some friends for a beer, an attempt to raise my spirits and remind me of what I *hadn't* given up. Chat turned to discussions of jobs and the expectations of bosses, of work/life balance and of the things these office-based workers all had in common. I wasn't much use in the conversation – the only time I'd configured an Excel spreadsheet was to work out which of the housebound needed visiting. Goldman Sachs it was not. I reflected that two hundred or so years ago, these friends who were now sitting around me would probably have been discussing theology or the politics of the Church but that was small comfort. In two hundred years' time would people even know what the Church was?

This sense of unease, this wilderness of the soul, pressed upon me during that first clerical Lent. Perhaps it was my fault. After all, I was no longer a disinterested observer from the pew. While that came with greater responsibility, greater glory – if being given the foil-wrapped biscuit instead of a custard cream at the end of the service counts as such – it also came with a greater sense of the pain of conflict, of complicity with failure, a much lonelier wilderness. I felt haunted by ghosts of clerics long dead and by some still, technically at least, alive. All those people who'd inspired me to take up the cloth, who had taught me what priestliness was meant to be. Was my self-indulgent misery failing them? Was it me, rather than the Church, who was at fault? Had I failed to love and long for the Lord? Had I, in this wilderness, not died to self as I had promised?

A final straw came one afternoon towards the end of Lent. Just as the busyness of Holy Week and Easter loomed, it transpired that, for about the third time that Lent, our plastic donation boxes, which stood by the front door, had been smashed in again and the few coins they contained nicked. The first few times I had taken it lightly. Was there a master criminal who went around wrenching the bobbing boats off RNLI boxes or trepanning those models of Guide Dogs for the Blind to get at the wealth of coppers within? I doubted it. Perhaps we were missing a trick and ought to roll out a donation point in the form of a fibreglass Justin Welby in every parish.*

However, this third time – amid the wilderness – the crime struck me differently. Those gifts were from people I knew and loved, many of whom struggled to afford even the few pounds they put in. They had placed their money there in trust that it would go to do good, and we who had asked it of them could no longer guarantee that.

---

* Or perhaps some shaped like the specific bishop would be more appropriate. Or simply the local vicar. The generous range of sizes among the clergy would present a problem, though. I know stick-thin clerics whose fibreglass selves would be full after a good carol service and others who might never be filled in a month of Sundays.

I stood by the boxes and fulminated angrily in the general direction of God. As I did so I noticed a man, a boy really, slip quietly into church behind me. Now when some people, especially men between the ages of eighteen and thirty-five, come into church and see a priest, they do an immediate about-face and leave. This one, though, was different. He saw me and wanted to talk, which he did, in an accent that revealed he was not originally from Liverpool. He told me he'd come up here for some sort of event, that he didn't really know anyone and that now he needed to go back south for a family funeral. I thought I knew what was coming next, but he looked at our smashed donation boxes, gave me a sad smile and simply asked me to pray for him. I promised I would and told him to wait there a moment, but by the time I had come back from my office with my wallet, he was gone. Back into a real wilderness, not my self-indulgent, self-constructed one.

I went out into the city to look for him but he had gone as quickly and quietly as he had arrived. I felt, once again, as if I'd failed. To cheer myself up I wandered into a well-loved newsagent and, almost without thinking, bought a scratch card with the money I'd intended to give away. As I shuffled in a daze past the crisps and tins of fizzy drink, I chiselled away at the covering with a fifty-pence piece and found underneath the requisite symbols to win ten pounds. I left the shop and found myself face to face with an old acquaintance. It was Chris, who, at the hospital, had so often been the recipient of scratch cards before Lenten rigour intervened. He told me how much they'd meant – not financially but as tokens of friendship. He was much better now, he said. 'I'm not quite out of the woods, but getting there.'

'Me too,' I said, and handed him the scratch card.

Lent, I learned, was not about acts to prove our self-righteousness or superhuman demonstrations of holiness but about finding beauty in the wilderness. Those Lenten wildernesses were not just spiritual Thunderdomes, as I had foolishly imagined, but moments, periods, places that each of us have to face.

My first Lent in holy orders hadn't been a very pious one – although I particularly enjoyed my roast lamb and cigar on Easter Day – but it had taught me about the true nature of the Lenten challenge. It had been – it remains – to keep the faith while in the wilderness, to keep up joy and laughter in the midst of a broken institution in a broken world. Yet the point of the wilderness is that it ends, and on the horizon looms Holy Week and Easter. Not just a moment for smoking two cigarettes and a cigar at once or biting into an enormous gummy cola bottle but a moment for hope.

II.

Bunions and the Resurrection

HOLY WEEK AND EASTER

Easter is one of the few times I can truly claim to have had an out-of-body experience. Not, I should clarify, one of those out-of-body experiences associated with religious ecstasy or the ingestion of hallucinogenic drugs but, rather, one of those associated with social embarrassment or farce. A moment where you can see, with visionary clarity, the chaos that is about to ensue but are frozen solid, powerless to stop it.

It was, properly speaking, the day before Easter Sunday, Holy Saturday.* It was night-time and a group of us were gathered on a small patio outside a church for the

---

* If your vicar is a pedant, annoy them by calling the Saturday before Easter Sunday, 'Easter Saturday'. It's actually 'Holy Saturday', with Easter Saturday being the day six days after Easter Sunday. However, nobody wants to buy Easter eggs then so it's moved forward a week in the popular imagination and wider parlance.

lighting of the Easter fire, traditionally the first ceremony of Easter. A large Easter or 'Paschal' candle is lit from it and carried into a totally dark church while the deacon chants, 'The light of Christ.' It's an enormously powerful declaration of the triumph of light over darkness, of life over death. It's also, like all the best things, a major fire risk.

I watched, helpless, as a fire that had begun as a gentle glow turned into a towering inferno helped by a combination of favourable wind and the fact that the vicar, who confessed he was 'fond of a good fire', had secreted an entire packet of firelighters amid the kindling. Every so often the blaze would seize upon some new artificial energy and swirl up fiercely. The unfortunate individual whose task it was to light the Easter candle leaned closer to the heat in an attempt to get the candle to light. He succeeded in setting his sleeve on fire, resulting in an unfortunate rapid striptease as the assembled company switched their priorities from saluting the Resurrection morn to preventing an accidental self-immolation.

This had happened some years before my time as a cleric, when I was just an eager, newish church attendee, one of those insatiable recent converts who wanted as much drama, as much ritual, as much unexpected setting on fire as he could get. Yet the scene still flashed in front of me at the high point of my first ordained Easter. As it was my turn to lower the candle, my brain flashed the image of *my* arm becoming engulfed by flame. What a way to crown my first year of being in holy orders it would have been.

But I've jumped ahead. Before we get to the joys of being engulfed by a celebratory fire, there's the rest of what we call Holy Week, the Great Week, the week when if you get more than a few hours' sleep you're doing well.* Palm Sunday, the week before Easter, is where it all starts. It's the day when congregations and clergy mark Jesus's triumphal entry into Jerusalem at the start of the very first Holy Week. I, in my naive enthusiasm, had suggested we might, as many churches do, procure the services of a donkey for some sort of re-enactment of that entrance. I was informed that we had in the past only for the beast to have got halfway along the aisle before defecating. It turns out that the clergy don't have quite the same animal-control skills as the Son of God. This information was imparted to me with a look that said, 'How sweet,' and 'Don't be a moron,' all at once. In retrospect, it was never a good idea: donkeys are not famed for their cooperative nature.†

Despite missing a donkey, Palm Sunday went ahead. The passion narrative, the story of Jesus's trial and crucifixion, was sung beautifully. The story retained its power. I managed to stub my toe on a pew during the procession out but, despite this minor hiccup, Holy Week had definitively begun.

---

* I confess this isn't one of the great ancient names the Church gives to Easter, but only because it would be even longer in Greek.

† Still, defecating donkeys are an improvement on an infamous pet blessing service where, midway through proceedings, a large dog succeeded in scaring a hamster to death.

Each year, the week continues in a similar vein. The services are a mix of the sublime, the dramatic and the very human. At its heart, Holy Week is about rhythm. It's the time of year when I'm at my most unequivocally 'High Church', the time when I pay closest attention to the outward form and function of what we do in services. In short, it's when the liturgy and its drama most enfolds and obsesses me. The rest of the week ran something like this.

Monday to Wednesday

These are days invariably spent fretting about the arrangements and organization for the 'big' events. It's always on these days that a church heating system fails or a particularly nasty bug spreads like wildfire among the clergy. During that first ordained Holy Week, no such unpleasantness occurred. Sermons were written, Easter eggs purchased, a particular giant gummy cola bottle was coveted. I chose to spend the time on those little bits of life admin that I knew I'd be too tired to do after the big event. On Tuesday I went to get my hair cut. 'Doing anything nice for the bank-holiday weekend?' the barber asked me. Of course I should have said, 'Yes! The best thing of all! I'll be proclaiming the conquest of life over death, the glories of the Resurrection!' but instead I mumbled, 'I'm working.' It's a generally accepted rule that it's best not to talk religion in the presence of scissors.

Maundy Thursday

If there is one day in the Church year when you should *absolutely* guarantee that you're wearing clean socks, it's Maundy Thursday. For the secular world, this is just the start of the Easter bank-holiday weekend but for churches it's when we celebrate the Last Supper, the meal Jesus had with his disciples before the crucifixion. At this meal, Jesus washed the feet of those who ate with him, as was the custom in Jewish hospitality at the time. This event is marked today by the clergy having to do the same thing to, well, anybody who shows up wanting an impromptu foot bath. Usually, this category is unsurprisingly quite small. If people want their feet manhandled they go to a podiatrist or a washing-up bowl filled with those tiny fish, not a vicar. Consequently, it is often the clergy who have to make up the numbers at the foot-washing ceremony in the Maundy Thursday service.

Aware that my own foot hygiene routinely leaves much to be desired, I planned ahead. At the start of the day I laid out an extra pair of socks in my flat with the intention that I would come back just before the service that evening, pre-wash my feet, cover them with talcum powder and slip gracefully into a pair of freshly laundered socks. I had hoped to give the impression to whichever colleague had the dubious task of washing the feet that I was a sweet-scented bastion of good foot care, rather than a rancid gremlin who routinely wore the same socks to the gym three days in a row.

Of course, my day didn't pan out as planned. I dashed across the city, on foot and in the rain, between meetings, allowing a particularly unpleasant build-up in my shoes. The meetings, inevitably, overran, meaning I had to dash back for the evening service, with no time to put my plan into action. To cap it all, I trod in an enormous brown puddle, soaking my right foot in all the goodness of urban rainwater.

Squelching and nervous, I processed down the aisle of the church for the service. The time came for the foot-washing, and a random assortment of parishioners (including some who'd been warned and had presumably had time to ensure their feet were nice and clean) took their seats as one of the assistant priests and I made our way round with a large bowl and a jug of carefully warmed water. Each person took off their clean shoe, removed a clean sock and presented a clean foot to be gently washed by the presiding priest, while I stood there, holding the jug and desperately hoping that someone would reveal a hoof or, at the very least, a bunion. It was not to be and, as we reached the end of the row of parishioners, the celebrant shot me a look, then peered at the final empty chair in the row. My time had come.

I sat down and removed my wet shoe with a squeak. I peeled off my still damp sock and plonked my foot down. A visible look of disgust greeted it. Still, I thought, at least I actually *needed* a foot-wash – and I sincerely doubt that those attending the Last Supper had made sure to get a pedicure prior to theirs. Sometimes, it occurred to me, rituals have practical uses as well as symbolic ones.

The service on Maundy Thursday finishes with a vigil. The body of the church is stripped of its decoration while the sacramental bread from Communion is placed on an altar decorated with lilies and lit candles. The clergy and congregation sit and wait, mirroring the watch in the Garden of Gethsemane just before Jesus's arrest. Our watch was briefly disrupted by a lily that wilted and was set alight by an adjacent candle, but the quick thinking of a congregant saw it dunked in the dirty foot-washing bowl. Slowly the congregation peeled away, leaving just the clergy and servers to pack up and begin the long journey towards the Cross.

Good Friday

After the rain that had played havoc with my Maundy Thursday, Good Friday broke in a burst of glorious sunshine. I'd hoped for a bit of pathetic fallacy, the day on which we remember the crucifixion being marked by a deluge or a thunderstorm or at least a cloud or two. Instead it was unseasonably warm, probably closer, in truth, to the weather on that first Good Friday in Jerusalem than the squall I had wanted.

The services on Good Friday are, as you'd expect, solemn in tone. The big service of the day is the devotion of the Three Hours, a liturgy devised in eighteenth-century Peru that somehow found its way to twenty-first-century Liverpool. The start involves three clergy – you'll see

that number games are a key part of constructing a service – lying on the floor for roughly three minutes.*
All well and good. Except that the unseasonal burst of clement weather that greeted our marking of the crucifixion had taken us and our heating system by surprise. It was, after all, mid-April in the north of England. The previous year, it had snowed. One could write a whole book about the vagaries and frustrations of church heating systems but unusually, due to the parish taking the courageous but expensive decision that it would be better occasionally to be too warm than for people to freeze to death inside, the church had a state-of-the-art underfloor heating system. Most days, this was a boon. *Most* days.

I went into the sacristy, the temperature of which already resembled that of the room next door to a kitchen where a particularly fierce chip-pan fire had broken out. There, Michelle, who was down to lead the service, looked at me, then at the layers of clothing we were about to put on and then at me again. Michelle was the longest serving of the clergy at the parish church. She had previously been a nun and was warm, no-nonsense and enormous fun. She didn't need to say anything as we both knew well enough that in a moment we were about to

---

* Biblical numerology – the study of how numbers relate to the practice of the Christian faith – is huge. From the authors of US crime thrillers to whole departments of the Vatican, the idea that certain numbers have meanings for Christians has long attracted both the devout and the deranged.

have to lie down, dressed in multiple layers, on a large and increasingly hot slab of stone. It would be like a treatment at a very prudish Turkish bath or a fully dressed hot-yoga session.

We processed in solemnly and, with great drama, fell to the floor at the foot of a wooden cross that had been placed on the altar. The floor was, as predicted, exceptionally warm. I looked to Michelle, who made a face and whispered, 'I may well have got down here but that doesn't mean I'll be able to get back up.' So there we lay, waiting, reflecting, sweating. In the event, after three minutes of me watching perspiration slide off my brow, we managed to get up and made a beeline to the row of vents in the floor where a quirk of the same heating system meant that a pleasing draught of cold air blew upwards. There was no repeat, thank goodness, of the Remembrance Day flashing.

There is a saying about Christ on the Cross: it was only love that kept him there. I think the same is probably true for clergy in the midst of the chaos and busyness of Holy Week. If anyone stopped and thought about what they were doing, they'd probably run a mile but love – of God and of the people they serve – keeps them there.

Later on that Good Friday, we observed the Stations of the Cross, a series of fourteen short readings and reflections telling of how Jesus went from being condemned to death to lying in the tomb. Each station was at a different part of the church. We moved to each in turn, pilgrims of all ages and backgrounds, shuffling in a holy conga line round the building. The procession was led by Father Bill, a kind and wise priest whose career in business had been set on a road to priesthood after the tragic death of his son. The moment he read of Mary's grief at meeting her son on his way to death on the Cross was intensely moving. It brought home how the pain of Good Friday resonates today, why its message of redemption for a fallen world remains so important for so many and why it's known as part of 'the greatest story ever told'.

So it was that each of us brought our pains, our tragedies, great and small, to the Cross.

Holy Saturday

I recall one priest telling me that Holy Saturday was the one day of the year he didn't answer the phone, indeed that it was the day when his priesthood was sort of 'on hold'. This was because 'It was the one day Nietzsche is right – God *is* dead.' Holy Saturday – not, as discussed, Easter Saturday – is the day the Church marks Christ lying dead in the tomb. Of course, in practice, the Church actually marks this pause, this uncomfortable moment of rest, with frenetic activity, mostly in preparation for Easter Sunday.

Liverpool, not a city known for its particular interest in what other people think to be conventional, marked it in a slightly different way. It was the custom for the Church of England and Roman Catholic communities to come together on a 'walk of witness' through the city centre, stopping at various points to pray and, with the assistance of a very large megaphone, remind the bank-holiday weekenders of the story of the Cross and Resurrection.

Amid the chaos of a thousand or so people from parishes across Merseyside, milling along a route a mile or so long, I was given the task of making things a little less chaotic. This seemed to consist of acting a bit like a sheepdog and hemming them in on one side when someone tried to make a break down a random side street or decided to pop into a shop and delay the progress of the entire procession while they sampled skin creams. To better achieve these goals, I tried to cultivate an air of detached authority, aided by my high-visibility jacket and black sunglasses. Halfway through, as I stood pompously surveying the crowd, a kindly older lady came up to me and took me by the arm.

'Is someone looking after you, love?' she asked sweetly. It soon transpired that she thought I was blind.

Easter Sunday

Easter is the moment when, for Christians, things are turned upside down. Life springs forth from death, victory is achieved through defeat, the human is taken up into the nature of the Divine. Appropriately for such a celebration of paradox, Easter Sunday begins, for many churches, on Saturday. So it is that we find ourselves back at the moment of my out-of-body experience as I watched my arm lurch closer and closer to the flame.

This time, no immolation occurred. The service on Holy Saturday is long, a vigil in the truest sense. Yet it, and the rest of Easter Sunday, passes in something of a blur, a little like our earliest years. I recall chanting, 'The light of Christ.' I recall the ringing of bells and lighting of candles. I can picture even now Louis's horrible giant cola bottle carved up after the vigil service and can still taste the illicit joy of a cigar in the early hours of Easter Monday, but compared to the planned intensity of the week before, Easter seems like a moment of beautifully detached release, a little like a dream. Then again, it is the celebration of new life – life quite unlike anything that has gone before. Perhaps a little blurring is no bad thing.

The cycle of life and death, the coming of the new, the mirroring of the daily or annual to the eternal is all part of the 'big picture' of the vicar-ing gig. Easter is no exception. Easter Sunday is the traditional day for baptizing new converts to Christianity. Having grown up with numerous siblings, all younger than me, I was aware of the institution of a new baby's christening even before I felt called to take faith a little more seriously. I would sit, trussed up in a very nineties jumper and some corduroys that spent the rest of the year in the back of my childhood wardrobe, and merrily kick the pew in front of me while whichever sister or brother was getting dunked that day was inducted into the new life of Jesus Christ.

Over the course of that first year I did more than my fair share of similar christenings, although now I was normally up front in a flowing robe rather than sitting at the back, abusing my relatives. At these services there were sleeping babies and there were screeching babies. There were babies who gurgled and smiled as the water was poured on their foreheads, and at least one who very obviously tried to lamp me as I trickled the carefully warmed water over his pate. There were babies dressed in the traditional long white christening gown, passed down from generation to generation, and one child whose parents wanted him baptized in a miniature Elvis suit.

Varied and occasionally oddly dressed though each child was, I found great joy in their christenings. Every one was welcomed into the community of faith, celebrated as loved not only by their adoring family but also by God. However, I came to realize that baptism was a much more multi-faceted event than the *de facto* first birthday party for a screaming or slumbering infant. Christenings can happen at any time and in any place. They happen in rivers and on hospital beds, by roadsides and on battlefields, at the beginning of a human life and just before the moment of physical death. The most moving baptism I attended that year was not one that I conducted.

It occurred while I was attending a Church conference for those who know and love the old-fashioned liturgy of the C of E, the Book of Common Prayer. These conferences, it will come as no surprise to learn, are often very odd affairs. They're not swanky business conferences, with companies and consultants hawking and pitching in some great exhibition hall. At this one, held

in the corner of a Cambridge college, I think the only
bits of trade paraphernalia I received were some adverts
for a Christian bookshop, a made-to-measure trouser
firm and a company specializing in selling fully serviced
second-hand cars to the clergy.

One of the speakers at the conference was the college
chaplain. At the end of his talk about poetics, he wondered aloud if he could ask us a favour. We were an odd
mix. I was there, in clericals and a donkey jacket, sitting
between a tweedy judge, with the most sonorous York-
shire accent I had ever heard, and a lady from Oxford
bedecked entirely in purple. The chaplain explained that
he'd been approached by a student who was from a country where Christians were persecuted. After much
deliberation, and despite the risks in returning home, he
had decided he wanted to be baptized. The thing was, it
was out of term. None of his friends were present. The
college was empty apart from this collection of enthusi-
asts. Would we, the chaplain asked, be the witnesses and
sponsors to the baptism of this student we had never
met? A cacophony of frail, often ignored voices echoed
unanimously: 'WE WILL.'

We processed to the chapel where the chaplain brought
the student to the font. He prayed for the Holy Spirit to
come down upon the gathering. When we were asked
whether we – the judge, the purple lady, a man with a
monocle, a woman with the most glorious smoker's bari-
tone, myself and all the rest of this rag-tag selection of
Christians – whether we would support and pray for this
nervous student, there was the most almighty response:

'WE WILL.' The chaplain poured the water on to the student's head, and wrinkled hands broke into spontaneous applause. As I watched a tear or two slip from the eyes around me, it was hard not to think that the Spirit *was* there, amid the beautiful incongruity. In a way it helped sum up Christianity in a single moment: this band of people were promising to care for one another, even strangers, and addressing someone they had never met before as 'brother'.

Even though baptisms are traditionally conducted at Easter, they are considered to be particular moments when the Holy Spirit is active and, of course, the Church has a special feast to celebrate the first coming of the Holy Spirit. In the Bible, the Book of Acts describes how people of various tribes and languages all came together to worship and passers-by assumed they were drunk. St Peter responded that they could not be drunk, for it was only nine o'clock in the morning. He might have been 'the rock on which Christ built his church' but he'd clearly never been to a theological training college the morning after Thursday 'party night'.* Forty days – another good biblical number – after the great feast of Easter we celebrate the feast of Pentecost, often known as Whitsun. By then the march towards summer has begun, recalcitrant church heating systems are switched off, and the risks of wearing black when out and about have become clear again. Of

---

* An absolutely miserable evening consisting of lots of church, a supper of soup and a rush to a local pub before closing time to drown the memory of it all.

course, the same Spirit that is called upon in baptisms at Easter and whose coming was mistaken for drunkenness in Jerusalem all those years ago was also what – or who – was called down upon me, a year before, during the sweltering service at the cathedral when I was ordained. As the feast of Pentecost drew near I reflected on what had changed for me, the Church, the world. The answer was everything and nothing. Nearly a year had passed and here I was again, sweltering, wondering about the coming of the Holy Spirit. What a year.

That's not quite fair. The summer before, when I was fresh in holy orders, tramping round the city in an uncomfortable new collar, I'd mostly been thinking about death. I'd been preoccupied by dying to self, dying to the past, dying from heatstroke. I suppose what that year – full of joy and disappointment, festivals, funerals, chaos and Christ – taught me is what I ought to have known all along: that death isn't an end but a beginning. That little death of ordination was an opening to a world where I met, worked with and, I hope, served the truly inspiring part of the Church, its ordinary people. Whether it was by a hospital bed or in a food bank or beside the font of a Cambridge chapel, whether I was being asked to bless betting apps on phones or (allegedly) criminal dogs or the final moments of a dying person, whether I was there in tears or in laughter, I was lucky enough to be in places where the Church still can be found, doing good and messing up and muddling along. Where, I suppose, that drunken, chaotic and loving Holy Spirit can be found too. The stiff cloth of my collar was a little more flexible now, a little more stained, too, as my parishioners used to delight in pointing out. In short, it was a little more human.

I suppose I'd learned, too, that everything is circular; and I don't just mean the collars. Being a young cleric wasn't about wearing the collar with pride or progressing to some next stage of my career. It was about coming up against the same moments – birth, life, death – over and over again and still failing. But failing with better humour, failing with a greater consideration of others, failing more Christianly each time. Each moment of death or failure, wherever it brought me into contact with love, the love of people and the love of God, was a gift. And realizing that death was, to quote one of the very greatest of Easter hymns, 'but the gate of life eternal'.* So, back to the start: why did I become a priest? Death, I suppose. And, to be fair, it has been much, much more fun than I ever could have imagined.

---

* The full opening line of the hymn is: 'Jesus lives! Thy terrors now, can, O Death, no more appal us'. Even apart from the absolutely pure heavy-metal energy of a hymn directly addressing and mocking death itself, it's got a cracking tune too. A certified Easter banger.

Epilogue

Fast forward. I have been ordained for some time now, it is summer again and, once more, I'm dealing with death. Nothing ever changes. This death, though, is different. I have moved on from Liverpool, to assist in a parish in London. I'm travelling from there on a (very) slow train into the depths of the Kent countryside to take a funeral. The funeral of my grandmother.

On arrival, I discover that I'm going to have to deal — or, more accurately, dice — with death in more ways than one. We were going to bring the coffin to the family home one last time before going to the church. I was thankful for the lessons learned about grief and ritual in that near-hotboxing incident at the very start of my ministry. A friend had agreed to drive me from the station into the depths of the countryside.

'I just happen to be in the area that day,' he had told me on the phone.

Now, in retrospect, I should have queried why someone who lived and worked on the other side of the country just happened to be in a particularly out-of-the-way spot in Kent, but part of being a cleric is learning to swallow odd or unusual information as if it were a day-to-day occurrence.

I was the only passenger to leave the train at the tiny village station. I lingered on the platform for a moment, looking up at the chipped paint on the name board and the hanging baskets gasping in the sun. My grandmother and I had taken numerous trains from that station, off on adventures far and wide. Now I was returning to it to send her off on the greatest adventure of all.

'Come on in!' my friend cried from the car. 'But just one word of warning. We're not alone.'

Possibilities raced through my mind: had he taken a mysterious Kentish lover? Did he have an imaginary friend or was he just using the royal 'we'? Or was a rural hijacker in the back seat?

'I'm in here with some bees.'

Oh, good.

Rural roads are dangerous at the best of times. Ill-kept, potholed, endlessly twisting and largely populated by speed addicts who are convinced they are the only people within three counties to possess a driving licence. The only thing that could make the usual helter-skelter journey through the Garden of England towards my grandmother's funeral more stressful would be filling the car with furious stinging insects.

There were four containers on the back seat, which meant we were sharing a car with a swarm of several thousand. One box clearly had a hole in it and so, as we veered around corners at speed, a succession of dazed and confused bees took out their disappointment at finding neither my friend nor I were pollen-rich flowers on my friend's exposed neck. I, miraculously, escaped with only one sting on my hand. Never have I been more thankful for that high, stiff piece of linen cloth that is the clerical collar.

Despite this unfortunate start, the funeral went well, a fitting send-off, the coffin surrounded by family in a beautiful church dappled with sunshine. I have seen enough final farewells to know a good one and this was, I think, one of the best. My grandmother was a remarkable woman, awkward at times, eccentric in her behaviour and opinions, but always, always loving. She taught me more than I could possibly have imagined, in ways I would never have thought of. And, above all else, she brought me, and many others, joy. Taking her funeral was a huge privilege, and I believe that the Resurrection means death isn't the end. Yet still, as I took the train back to London, between Marden and Paddock Wood, I wept. The price, I suppose, of love.

Plenty of things about life as a cleric give cause to weep. I always wondered why we were historically known as 'men of the cloth'. I now know it's because we spend most of our time touching it.* Failure and frustration are constant companions. By all external (and, indeed, most internal) Church of England measurements my Church 'career' has been a failure. I have failed to find any permanent job – that most recent ministry in London has been as an unsalaried stand-in, doing dogsbody work in return for a house but no pay. A sort of zero-hours contract for vicars. While serving there I discovered that for all the kind and good clerics, like Crispin, Bill and Michelle, a

---

* There are, of course, now 'women of the cloth' too. My experience is that they are often much better at holding all these fears and frustrations together with good, prayerful, kind ministry than we insecure men are.

minority are manipulative and abusive, uninterested and duplicitous. Most clergy and lay people in the Church of England are trying their hardest to live and love to the best of their ability, but no institution is perfect nor the people in it. After I left Liverpool, I encountered clerics who delighted in sidelining their juniors or volunteers, those who were sweetness to people's faces, then dealt in calumnies behind their backs, those who would preach about the poor, then do their best to ignore them *in situ*. It was often depressing, but all sorts of people become vicars. As I finish writing this book even that appointment is coming to its unhappy end. As it stands I have failed, in the Church's own words, to find enough 'experience' to justify another post. My new diocese has told me there is nowhere for me at the moment and so I am, I hope temporarily, leaving ministry. I'm not sure I mind. I have found out things about myself of infinite value and, I hope and trust, have served others in the spirit of my calling. If the Church of England doesn't think that's a good thing, it's on them.

Just as I'm finishing this book, I find myself taking what will be, for a while, my last funeral. I'm filling in at a parish where there is no vicar but I'm not considered up to scratch to take it on full time. I'm in limbo, taking services but unable to make real connections. As such, my contact with the family of the deceased was limited. In brief conversations with the next of kin I learned that he was a reserved, gentle man, whose main hobbies were an enthusiasm for Georgian architecture and collecting harpsichords. His passion was his professional life, so a colleague had been asked to give a eulogy on his contribution to cardiology.

The link raised a hint of recognition. I had been born with a serious heart condition, so much so that I was baptized as a newborn not in a church but in a fruit bowl at home, just before I went into hospital. Open-heart surgery on a baby of that age is a tricky, tragic thing. My parents had selected the teddy bear with which I was going to be buried. I still have him, kept in a cupboard owing to my own vanity and pretensions to adulthood. He's difficult to explain as a memento mori. The link to a heart doctor registered but then, as I hope this book has shown, I have commended many people to God whose lives could conceivably have touched my own: soldiers who served with my father; patients treated by my mother; and, of course, countless children of the same God who knew and loved those places dear to me.

As the eulogy progressed, it became clear that this connection was a deeper one. Dr Derek Gibson was the father of the physiological echo and had made possible, in particular, its use in congenital cases. He had been a stalwart at the Royal Brompton Hospital, where my surgery and the preparations for it had taken place; he knew those corridors along which I'd been wheeled when small. They'd always seemed so cavernous to me: long and whitewashed, like the nave of a Dutch church. Dr Gibson's energy, research and fierce intelligence had advanced cardio-technology in leaps and bounds. With each leap, lives had been saved. Lives like mine.

Afterwards, as we stood outside in the crisp January air, a mourner came up to me. I recognized the face instantly for I had stared up into it over many bored hours of medical procedure. Manjit Gosen had been a pupil of Dr Gibson, and had also been my paediatric echo cardiographer. I can still remember his cold hands and the Thomas the Tank Engine noises he would make to cover the strange yell of the machine as it scanned my heart. He'd recognized my name, preposterous as it is, from the order of service. 'I knew you were either a patient,' he told me, 'or an international rugby player.'

We chatted and reminisced about the Brompton – those corridors again – and about the echo, the things it had made possible, and the man who had been responsible for them.

'Do you think he saved my life?' I asked.

'Yes,' Manjit said, 'he probably did.'

It was a moment of circularity. A bridge between two lives across the decades. A moment that linked life with death, adulthood with infancy, the start of my ministry to what might well be the end of it. After all, if death had made me become a priest, it seemed a fitting enough ending.

My ministry – for it is that and definitely *not* a 'career' – brought me into contact with the true treasures of the Church. Not its silver plate or its procedures or its pomp or its promotions but its people. The privilege of knowing and loving them: the strange, awkward, wonderful, *holy* people, who, despite all the Church throws at them, still come to it in search of love. They're the ones who run the practical expressions of love on the ground – the Sunday clubs and schools, the food banks and outreach programmes. And they're the ones who, even more importantly, point us, point me, in the direction of a love that is even greater. And, above all else, they have brought me joy.

Acknowledgements

This is manifestly a book about people, so it seems only right that I should thank some of them for their enormous contributions. First, I thank everyone at Liverpool Parish Church, where I spent what may prove to be the happiest years of my life. In particular, I thank those great models of priesthood: Crispin, Bill, Michelle, Yazid, Ray and Louis. Also Jean, Sue, Roger, Peter, Jim, Peter, Eva, Pauline and countless others, for their infinite patience with my incompetence and regular administration — especially in Peter's case — of high-proof spirits. I owe a huge debt of gratitude to the bishops of that diocese, Paul and Bev. I must also acknowledge the support of my family, my cell group of Andy, Dan, Nick and Ben, and my non-clerical friends, who have kept me sane(ish) at various points: George, Dan, Chris, Simon, Tom, Aidan, Alex, Ed, Ellis and Annie. My thanks, too, to Alex and Max for getting this show, finally, on the road. Thanks also to Gus Brown, Hazel Orme, Kate Samano, Beci Kelly, Phil Evans, Patsy Irwin, Sara Roberts, Oliver Grant, Tom Lloyd-Williams, Allison Warren, Kayla Grogan and Kaleigh Choi, for all their hard work on making the book a reality. To my spiritual director, David, who listened to hours of moaning. And, finally, to Madeline, for her constant love and support. Thank you all.

The Reverend Fergus Butler-Gallie is a writer and priest who has ministered in parishes in Liverpool and Central London. He grew up amid a large family of maniacs, was then educated at the universities of Oxford and Cambridge, and has spent time living and working in the Czech Republic and South Africa. He is the author of the bestselling *Times* and *Mail on Sunday* Book of the Year *A Field Guide to the English Clergy* and the *Spectator* Book of the Year *Priests de la Resistance!* (both published by Oneworld). He speaks regularly on radio and has written numerous articles for *The Times*, *Independent*, *Guardian*, *Church Times*, *The Critic* and *The Fence*.